risking utopia

on the edge of a new democracy

irshad manji

Douglas & McIntyre
VANCOUVER/TORONTO

FOR MY MOTHER, AND ANYONE ELSE WHO LOVES CONVERSING

Douglas & McIntyre
1615 Venables Street
Vancouver, British Columbia
V5L 2H1

Canadian Cataloguing in Publication Data

Manji, Irshad
  Risking Utopia

  Includes bibliographical references and index.
  ISBN 1-55054-434-9

  1. Political participation—Canada. 2. Populism—Canada.
I. Title.
JC599.C3M36 1997   323'.042'0971   C96-910839-7

Cover design by Marian Lucas Lane
Text design and typesetting by Val Speidel
Printed and bound in Canada by Best Book Manufacturers, Inc.
Printed on acid-free paper

The Future written by Leonard Cohen. Copyright 1993 Leonard Cohen Stranger Music, Inc.
Used by permission. All rights reserved.

The publisher gratefully acknowledges the assistance of the Canada Council and of the British Columbia Ministry of Tourism, Small Business and Culture.

CONTENTS

INTRODUCTION

shift happens

This book is about an unexpected journey. I began as a feminist determined to mount an unapologetic defence of her movement. But shift happened. I ended up as a citizen, someone who sees more value in the messy trade-offs of democracy than in the tidy absolutes of dogma. Along the way, I—and my world—got layered.

Where I began is not unlike the story of many young North American women. I came to feminist activism after watching my mother endure a miserable twenty-four-year marriage and a stigma-stained divorce. At age eighteen, desperate to work through my rage at my dad (for having treated his wife and kids like dirt), my mum (for not leaving him sooner) and myself (for not having the answers), I crashed a meeting of the Vancouver Society on Immigrant Women.

After listening to their stories and having mine heard, I started to think beyond the traditional bounds of "women's issues." Some of these women had been unemployed for years despite their two university degrees. Some had been juggling part-time jobs for a decade or more. Their driving issues necessarily differed from those of the elegant agitators who shaped my image of North American feminism: the women who battled for seats in corporate boardrooms and tee-off times at all-male golf clubs. Such struggles matter, but the testimonies of immigrant women broadened my picture of feminism's fight.

They also forced me to reconsider my anger towards my mum. She speaks six languages and works for an airline company—not translating, but cleaning. As children, my two sisters and I had to spend holidays without her because those days paid time and a half; insurance for a woman whose job was forever being jeopardized by racial harassment. Besides logging as many hours as she could, my mum usually joined in her co-workers' taunts of "tar baby" and "spear chucker" so the boss would see her as a team player. Almost anything to avoid the pink slip. I now understood that my mum's limited choices delayed her decision to end an abusive relationship.

Only then did it occur to me that tackling racism had to be part of my conviction as a feminist. If one abuse of power opens the gate to another, then sexism cannot be defeated in a vacuum. Moreover, as long as race claims a place in my fight, so must class, sexual orientation, physical (dis)ability—all dimensions of our complicated human selves.

So I set out to prove that feminism is the way to rid society of unwarranted discrimination. I pored over books, attended conferences, observed women's studies classes and hung out with veteran activists. That is when my doubts started simmering about feminism as the sole answer to humanity's ills.

I define feminism as the belief that all human beings, beginning with women but not ending there, deserve the power to make dignified choices. Yet this idea sounded laughably naive once I put it to the test with other feminists. Suspicion, even scorn, came my way when I asked some feminists to back up their certitudes that "most straight people are homophobes," "the original homophobes are white men" and "men's sexist, racist structures must be demolished."

"Whose side are you on, anyway?" was the usual snap response to my requests for explanation.

This leery impatience reflected a larger, equally acrimonious and ongoing slugfest over the direction of North American feminism. In the blue trunks: the dissident feminists. In the red: the orthodoxy. In taking issue with violence statistics, invocations of "backlash" and "oppression," the emergence of lesbian-of-colour caucuses and the like, the ascending dissident feminists have spouted hyperbole, ignoring their own call for tolerance, accuracy and balance. Their targets, the orthodox feminists, have volleyed back vitriol, making a mockery of their women-loving, peace-nurturing oratory. Neither camp has cared to learn from the other. After following enough exchanges of rhetorical blows, my doubts swelled. Could I defend feminism without apology?

Meanwhile, it struck me that moderate women did not have a clue, much less a concern, about how their "common sense" feminisms excluded others. They insisted that there is no crime in being white, middle-class and feminist. I agreed. What has to change, I learned, is the white, middle-class *mind-set* of feminism, because that mind-set assumes too much and addresses too little for countless women and men.

These tensions, colliding with the increasingly conservative politics of our time, pointed me towards a brand-new question: How can we all experience belonging in a world that is losing its visible borders yet replacing them with the invisible walls of mistrust, cynicism and hatred? Feminism, I had found, was not immune. I had to reach beyond it.

My initial agenda—justifying a troubled feminism—matured into a project: fostering an ethos of belonging that encourages everyone to be a participant before labelling anyone a deviant. Whether in the feminist movement or in society at large, the challenge is to belong.

Still, my hope for belonging continues to spring from feminism. Its boundaries have opened up as I have grown up. From what I have watched of its evolution, this movement can inform a vision of democracy.

Inform democracy—but not supplant it. Today, the feminist movement is grappling with the dilemmas of democracy that our entire planet faces. In particular, the impulse to maintain order jostles with the desire to dispense freedom. Feminists not only embody this polarity, we can be madhouse mirrors of it. That is the second reason for using the movement as a prism through which to view the riddles of belonging.

Although feminism served as the compass of my journey, the detours, potholes and crossroads produced the most moving surprises. One moment remains vivid. It started when the phone rang.

"Hi *jaan* [sweetheart]."

"Hi Ma," I replied. "What's up?"

"I'm okay. Just a little upset."

"Why?" I groaned, thinking: All right, which pair of sweaty socks did my sister's boyfriend leave lying around the house this time?

"Everyone's talking about you at the mosque in Montreal. Somebody saw you on TV saying that you're Muslim and gay, and that Allah [God] says that's fine. Did you say that?"

"Well," I sputtered, "I didn't say that *exactly*. People love to twist words. But, yeah, I did talk about it on TV."

"I'm just curious," my mum continued. "I'm not judging you, but why do you have to go on TV and talk about the way you are? If you were more like us—I'm not saying 'normal,' okay, I'm saying 'like us'—you wouldn't say it on TV, right? So why do you have to talk about it in public? It's nobody's business."

A thousand and one arguments raced through my head, and I lunged for almost all of them. "You don't have to say you're straight because that's considered the norm, so others expect it. Should I pay the price for their refusal to accept new things? … This isn't just about me. What about all those gay Muslim kids out there who are silently suffering right now and need to know someone's on their side? … So few openly queer people have access to the media; unless gays and lesbians come out in every forum available to us, the smug straight world can deny our existence … You're assuming that sexuality is only about what someone does in bed, but there's a lot more to it. Sexuality helps define how we see human beings—for everything they are or for the small part that society can bear to acknowledge? … There's no shame in difference; we'd be boring without it … Hey, did you know that the Pope said, 'We should not fear the truth about ourselves'?" Blah, blah, blah.

I flailed about to avoid addressing my mum's unspoken question. She was not asking me why I had done it, but how I could have. For this, I had no ready response.

Towards the end of my grab-bag defence, my voice grew shaky. "Don't cry," my mum counselled. "I'm not upset with you. I'm upset with those gossips. All they do is whisper. They should have the guts to talk to me or you about it."

Just like my mum was doing. "You know me," she joked. "No matter what, I have to tell you how I feel and what I think. I have to be honest with you." She said she trusted me to make the right decisions and asked only that I remember my family. We hung up.

In a five-minute conversation, years of bumper-sticker indoctrination washed away. Left behind was a radiant shade of grey, her truths blended with mine. I realized that we cannot be individuals alone; our actions always have consequences for others. At the same time, I realized that I care about my mum's experiences, opinions and feelings, and therefore about her complexity as an individual. An ethos of belonging might be born of labels, but it makes room for communication.

When militant ideology shielded me, everything looked like another choreographed step in the repertoire of sexism, racism and homophobia. Since then, I have accepted that human beings are bundles of contradictions living in an imprecise, interdependent world. I once sought coherence at the cost of creativity; today the most coherence I can muster is a politic, to borrow historian Gordon Wood's description of liberalism, that deepens our capacity "to relate to strangers, to enter into the hearts of even those who [are] different."

My liberalism draws its greatest insights from the strangers I met on this journey, who did invite me to relate. Resisting either/or thinking, they showed me how a voluntarily veiled woman can understand a crusader for toplessness, how a campus women's centre can welcome men, how a teacher can share power with his students, how the "white way" of schooling can help an aboriginal woman stand up to repressive native elders, how a couple can be both unmarried and committed to their nuclear family, how a disabled, bisexual daughter can simultaneously appreciate and question her mother's sanitized image of her, and how a journalist can take daily responsibility in the mass media.

These young paradoxes, whom I tracked down on three Canadian coasts and spots in between, testified to the possibilities of turning alienation into meaningful participation. They demonstrated how to be citizens of a potentially borderless planet. The result, for me, was a series of unpredictable discoveries. Values really do count. Self-interest, too, can be a source of progressive action. Above all, because they have to try harder than most to belong, those on the edge of society often exude a spirit of democracy from which we can all learn. I did.

Such twists led me to the Utopia of Complexity. Rather than pursue perfection or imagine the fantastic, this utopia makes the best of what we already have—flux, mystery and diversity. To squeeze the most from these attributes of pluralism, the Utopia of Complexity pushes democracy to be one giant bazaar where we may all bargain for belonging. Here, citizens shed the protective armour of prejudice and brace for the unanticipated lessons of engaging each other as compatriots and thus as civic equals. But even in this utopia, the most profound riddle of belonging remains.

Journeys bestow a gift greater than answers—questions. On my quest, I ask: How do we honour individual uniqueness without losing

respect for common purpose? Can I champion a set of ethics and not vio-
late my passionate belief in plurality of perspective? What is it to be radical, remembering that the earth can be rigid but that it can be amazingly
flexible too? Could the Utopia of Complexity debut in Canada?

Although utopias have an end-of-history feel, the point of this one is
not the safety of the arrival but the adventure of the travel. Hence my
final question: Why reach for a utopia that is more of a risk than a retreat?

. I .

division

"I love ... the image of the Indian goddesses with 40 arms. Now nothing is more powerful in symbolizing that at any one point in time a fully human person is 40 things at once. Your identity is not a linear identity. Your identity is not a monolith. You are complex, you are many things in one, and those many things are constantly partly at struggle, partly in harmony, shaping the 'you' that is. The complexity of imagery is what I look into the past for, and I think it's needed because we are living — in imaginative terms — in a highly impoverished period."

—Eco-feminist Vandana Shiva,
The World Transformed, 1995

"I'm vulnerable to identity changes because I'm desperate to find a niche. I'm like Crystal Pepsi."

—Twenty-something cyber-genius Daniel Underwood,
in Douglas Coupland's Microserfs, 1996

CHAPTER 1

on being white trash: a first look at belonging

Many refer to me as a Muslim Lesbian Feminist. Labels are simple; the politics behind them are anything but. I cannot deny being an observant Muslim, a committed queer or a practising feminist, yet with each label comes a set of assumptions that, if explored further, would be punctured.

She must be a socialist. My love of initiative colours me solidly capitalist. At twelve years old, I ran a lucrative lunch business out of the class cloakroom. My few months of operation made me important to my peers. They made me popular. They made me $75.

If she is lesbian and feminist, she hates men. When I came out to my mother, she pleaded with me not to give up on guys. "Give up on guys?" I thought to myself. "Is she kidding? I'm telling her (and everyone else) I'm a lesbian because bisexuality gets no respect." A shame, that. To be pressed against throbbing muscle, enveloped by arms that I can bite but rarely dent, separated merely by a sheet of sweat and a lick of latex, exchanging grunts and grins, all the while knowing he can have me but he cannot keep me: Mum is in luck. That is too good to give up.

She wallows in victimhood. To be a victim is to be immobilized by circumstance, a situation I have always shunned. Even when it meant behaving like a jerk. In a teenage act of pure, lip-smacking spite, I spread a rumour about a friend who had become a born-again Christian. Cautiously passed notes told classmates that I had spotted her hugging a girl. My anonymous phone calls to her home began, "Hey, lezzie, you're being watched." I felt a perverse power surge in singling somebody out. After years of being called a Paki, I was finally showing these missionaries of the supremacist Messiah that I could give as good as I got. To hell with volunteering victimhood for the sake of sisterhood.

She is vegetarian. I adore my burgers, fries and cheese doodles. "Have your eggplant," I exhort my girlfriend. "Be one with the soil, babe. I choose to be one with the oil." After deconstructing my diet—problematizing my patties and contextualizing my cole-slaw—the post-modernists at my table can only deem me White Trash. Fine, I nod. White Trash captures me better than Muslim Lesbian Feminist.

Identity starts with labels such as Muslim Lesbian Feminist. But when you make the effort to lift my label and ask questions—"You don't eat meat, do you?"—you give me the right to be acknowledged and the responsibility to refine or replace your perceptions: "Not only do I eat meat; this dyke devours Whoppers." Rooted in caring sufficiently to be sufficiently curious, that interaction is the mark of belonging. Identity thus emerges from our dialogue, your perceptions meeting mine.

On their own, labels serve as security blankets. They can insulate us when everything else seems to be eroding in the sweep of economic, cultural and technological change. But also like blankets, labels often restrict movement and conceal the real goings on underneath. I hope for a world where we turn over the labels and investigate; that is the genesis of belonging.

I understand the advantage of using labels. They are things to which people can react. We all attach ourselves to groups, or are attached to them, as a point of departure for further expression. It is when labels clamp communication that belonging is in jeopardy. By belonging, then, I do not mean unconditional acceptance, better known as mindlessness. Belonging is a state in which we accept each other just enough to explore.

The question of belonging is complex not only because of the extent to which I want others to accept me but also because of the extent to which I am willing to accept them—their fears no less than their foods. Each of the anecdotes above reflects my lifelong struggle to ensure mutual belonging. Even as a child, I knew that the burden of belonging began with me. To improve my chances of finding a niche, however fleeting, I could not allow myself to feel powerless. I had to grab the opportunity to play lunchtime Santa, bully someone vulnerable or disclose my not-so-straight self. Assimilation is passive, belonging active.

But my endeavours since childhood have proven that fighting like hell to be in the game satisfies only one side of the belonging equation. Belonging is a contract in which the dominant culture—of a classroom, a workplace, a society—meets the conditions of human dignity so that it may benefit from the continued contributions of those it dignifies. Put bluntly, the other side of the belonging bargain is the treatment you get once in the game.

An immigration officer introduced me to that contract when, in October 1972, he refused to settle my family in Montreal. After nationalist dictator Idi Amin seized power in our native Uganda, thousands of Asians were given only days to choose between leaving or dying. With no time to brush up on world geography, my family fled, eventually landing in Montreal. The immigration officer asked my parents why we wanted to live in that city. Desperate not to blow our big chance, my French-speaking mother replied that Montreal begins with the same letter as the family name, so it might make for a happy fit. Upon surveying me and my sisters, the officer told my mother that we would not survive the coming Montreal winter—we were dressed for tropical weather. He offered us Vancouver instead. A few stamps later, the family was bound for the other side of the country.

In retrospect, I would have loved to grow up in a bilingual city. But the officer's move showed that he was paying attention. There is no doubt he had power over us. Even so, this symbol of state hegemony, this gatekeeper of cheap labour, cared enough to view refugee children as human beings with a Canadian future rather than labels lost in a ditched past. He cared enough to wonder what we needed. "A society in which strangers would feel common belonging and mutual responsibility to each other depends on trust," explains Canadian philosopher Michael Ignatieff in his trenchant 1984 book-length essay *The Needs of Strangers*. "[A]nd trust in turn reposes on the idea that beneath difference there is identity."

I doubt that trust would be accorded my refugee family in 1997. The last few years have seen this country suffocate newcomers with suspicion. A federal law requires the finger-printing of refugee claimants. A $975 "right-to-land" fee—the equivalent of a decade's work in areas of the Third World—has been introduced to help sustain the social services used by immigrants (a line routinely rehearsed by politicians and bureaucrats on the evening news. Still, studies conclude that, through taxes, most immigrants give the government far more money than they borrow.) Iron handcuffs and leg shackles adorn some refugees who are kept in crowded Canadian detention centres for months, despite being charged with no crime and, occasionally, despite being as young as thirteen. A prime minister pitching the "politics of inclusion" creates the Ministry of Public Security to "handle" immigrants and refugees. The label implied and imposed by all of these measures: THREAT. Public opinion apparently agrees. Belonging is in jeopardy.

Why would collective interaction be dying now? French diplomat Jean-Marie Guéhenno identifies the single biggest factor in the title of his 1995 book *The End of the Nation-State*. For two hundred years, the distinct territorial integrity of nation-states cultivated common bonds among diverse groups of people, in Europe first and across much of the world later. Today, as institutional and geographic borders lose their legitimacy, our search for belonging intensifies. But taking the place of those borders are the less visible tentacles of technology—microchips, lasers, cables. Materials for digital compatability, they are not yet the stuff of social solidarity.

More insidious are the psychological borders being erected by anxiety. When technological networks displace territorial boundaries, and economic trade pacts subvert the independence of elected governments, people are thrown into uncertainty, prompting many of us to seek assurance, any assurance, from just about anywhere. At the close of the twentieth century, writes Guéhenno, the battles of religion, race, tribe and ideology are "defensive reflexes. They express a turning inward, a fear of the vast world that escapes us, and from which we cannot escape." Reflex trumps reflection, bolstering mental barricades that incarcerate imaginations, promote agendas over visions and leave belonging with barely a fighting chance.

In Canada, witness the fundamentalisms now flourishing among the so-called Left and Right. To appease our uncertainties, hyper-ideologues present us with simplistic solutions to human conundrums. The spasm of the hour, neo-conservatism, permits belonging under very limited conditions. Contrary to its freedom-fawning language, this ideology (like all revolutionary creeds) demands conformity. You must pay taxes to be a legitimate citizen. Families must be traditionally structured to be worthy of tax breaks. Armed with tax breaks, citizens are compelled to consume. Upon buying a TV, consumers receive a "bill of rights." The implication? Those who cannot afford to enter an electronics shop do not deserve the new citizenship. In my province of Ontario, these are the crucial links in

Premier Mike Harris's "Common Sense Revolution." A stubborn exercise in social engineering, the revolution lets little slip from its authority.

Yet as the new Right hardens its authority, the old Left seems to be responding in kind. Moral absolutes are being met with more absolutes. Consider the words of Judy Rebick, one of Canada's most prominent left-wing pundits and former president of the National Action Committee on the Status of Women. In a November 1995 speech, she argued for democratizing our institutions. I applauded. She insisted that young people will never join a movement or party in which they know they will not be heard. Hear, hear, I whispered. And she called on progressives to indulge in a little self-criticism before dumping all over our opponents. But then, Rebick returned to the canon of absolutes. Paraphrasing Leon Trotsky, she declared Ontario's future as "a choice between socialism and barbarism." She proclaimed it "crap" to think that all people should be served by a social democratic government. "This is a class-divided society," Rebick expounded, "and a New Democratic Party should govern for the working class, the poor and the oppressed, not for the business class," as if entrepreneurs and their employees have nothing to do with each other. Above all, she suggested that the more extreme the Right becomes, the further Left the rest must lurch.

Although I have long admired Rebick's work, I cannot swallow her stark conclusions. They infantilize progressive politics. To those who are anti-choice, life begins at conception. It is not so cut and dried for pro-choicers. Similarly, however you cook the books, one more penny earned than spent is a profit. But "equality," a goal instinctively mouthed by progressive activists, is much more ambiguous, not to mention ambitious. Equality defies easy definition, and cannot be neatly packaged without verging on immaturity. Rebick's fulminations amount to little more than an unchanted slogan: Our fundamentalism is better than their fundamentalism. To my mind, fundamentalism of any stripe discriminates impulsively, kills possibilities and finally thwarts belonging.

Even if times of complexity demand some generalization for the sake of clarity, the question must be asked: Clarity in whose interest? Surely not that of citizens. In their inflated appeals to our emotions, revolutionaries entice us to feel more than think; to love and hate and not waste much breath on those who evaluate. This impatience cannot serve the cause of civic interaction.

Nor, of course, is it intended to. Rather, contrived clarity caters mostly to the media. To a degree, I sympathize. In a political culture that makes judges out of journalists and juries out of focus groups, your perspective is presumed not to exist if it does not get publicity. And if you take more than a couple of sentences to explain your perspective, prepare to pucker up. Nuance is the kiss of death for wide coverage, which means the ideological assurances sought by the anxious masses will not reach them. Which, in turn, means that the masses will not be mobilized for revolutionary change.

That is if you bank on a major assumption: however dog-lazy our media, tossing it a juicy label will arouse interest in poking underneath for some grasp of who that label is intended to represent. When the label enjoys enough such publicity, and thus familiarity, it will exude the warmth of an identity.

I am not convinced. Think of the blockbuster label "Generation X." For all the ink and air time devoted to it, the mass media has barely touched the intriguing politics behind the way the label is applied. Had they investigated, journalists might have seen that the label does not represent an immense slice of North America's young people.

Gen X generalizations have been popularized through the perspectives of those who grew up expecting fairness and balance as the natural order of things; those who believed their transition from adolescence to adulthood would be characterized by a steady, even uncomplicated, inclusion into the System; those for whom belonging was supposed to be a birthright, not a battle. Recall the theme song to the twenty-something sitcom *Friends*; it begins by affirming that nobody warned us about false promises and postponed progress. But, as a kid of colour living in North America, nobody *had* to tell me it would be this way. For me, belonging has always been a negotiation, not an entitlement.

For the longest time, I went by the nickname "Pinky" because it was less troublesome for my classmates to pronounce than "Irshad." Rather than accept being invisible to them, I made it more convenient for them to acknowledge me. What did I get for my compromise? Chants of "Ink, Pink, you stink, riding on a horse's dink." Understood, kids are primitive egalitarians. They will milk the most from anyone's handicaps. Name-twisting, in particular, must be a worldwide phenomenon among seven-year-olds.

But this situtation was different. It did not involve a name that my parents had unlovingly dictated to me, but one that I had taken for the love of strangers. I tried to ease their lives, and they exploited that to make mine harder. Fairness and balance as the natural order of things? Try again.

Which is precisely what I did. In junior high school, I sometimes pre-empted being slurred as a Paki by denying my actual lineage and announcing that I came from the Middle East. As a Muslim, I had the right religion to claim Arab origins. My timing was good, too: Muslims had not yet been baptized the post-communist scapegoats.

A decade of delaying, downplaying and denying: this was my reality long before Douglas Coupland legitimized low expectations and little security in *Generation X*, his 1991 novel about three young under-employed friends who run away from the real world and retreat to a Palm Springs bungalow in their search for belonging. The media lapped up the label. When young people of colour agonize over their place in North America, that is minority angst. But when white youth struggle to make sense of their place, that, by sheer numbers, is a social phenomenon. To the reporters, it is worth documenting. To the marketers, it is worth hawking. Generation X has become one of the hottest phrases of the 1990s.

One of the most distorted, too. Journalists and advertisers have assumed that young people of colour must be part of the Gen X set because its defining traits are age, anger and economic exploitation, right? Wrong, Coupland reminded in a 1995 "eulogy" for his concept of Generation X. Writing in *Details* magazine, he pointed out that it is their deliberate withdrawal from society, their drift to the fringe for the sake of sanity, which epitomizes Xers. Seen in this context—a context that the media missed entirely—many young people of colour cannot be Xers even if we want to be. Some-times we volunteer our moves to the margin; more often, we are pushed.

Like the young aboriginal woman who, after trying to apply for a job in person, came home and got on the phone. " 'Hello, Tim Hortons Donuts? I am inquiring about your advertisement for a job. Yes. Is it still available? It is. Well, asshole, why did you tell me it was filled?' "Her next call was to a human rights commission. Whatever the toll on her sanity, she had to find a way of staying in the game.

Contrast her to the bartender in *Generation X*. Bored and bitter after a shift at his McJob, he interrupts a conversation to hop across the street and vandalize a car. He would argue that he was provoked; the car's bumper sticker boasted: "We're Spending Our Children's Inheritance." Imagine the aboriginal woman getting away with that excuse to damage property—especially if she went out of her way to do so, like the bartender.

Consciously or not, the authentic Xer understands that his expression of anger will be better tolerated than, say, a native woman's. He knows that people who come from a place of relative security are perceived to be less deserving of punishment, burdening people without that privilege to be more circumspect in how, and how much, they express. Consequently, vandalism is a luxury for those Xers who, if nothing else, can look forward to the security of inheriting their parents' mortgage-free homes down the road. Kids in urban housing developments—"rat-renters," as some call themselves at Toronto's Regent Park complex—cannot lay the same claim to eventual ownership. For them, as for the aboriginal woman, voluntary marginalization would be a bogus pose.

As such, the roots of resentment among many young people of colour run deeper than the Gen X label suggests. To misunderstand this or, worse, not to care, is to stifle the possibilities for genuine belonging. Playing to the mass media carries that price. In their hunt for crisp conflict and digestible optics, the media want to create fixed identities. Yet the essence of identity lies not in what is fixed but in what is fluid.

That is why a label is not an identity; it is the runway en route to identity, the static strip from which we literally take off. People assume labels or pin them onto each other for simplicity's sake. So whether we fully accept our prepackaging must always be up for discussion. Belonging, the cornerstone of identity, begins with that discussion.

Thus, my identity is not merely about who I think I am. That would be self-perception. Identity is also about who (or what) others think I am. This need to involve others is especially important where I am facing a dominant culture—in a workplace, on a campus, even in a family. In each case, the metaphor of belonging as a contract makes sense: I take the responsibility to bend in exchange for the right to belong. There is no shame in bending. It gets me further than allowing myself to be captive behind the bars of an imposed tag.

Is a label inclusive or confining if it is based on assumption? That should be asked not only of the label "Xer" but also of "feminist." Indeed, I started questioning the feminist movement when I recognized the parallels between its history and the making of the Gen X myth. Just as Generation X draws inspiration from the realities of white youth, with youth of colour presumed to share those realities, so feminism was organized on the truths of many white women but presumed applicable to all women.

Take feminism's bedrock belief in reproductive choice. During the 1960s and '70s, feminist leaders figured they were promoting every woman's choices by pressing for abortion on demand. They neglected North America's history of forcibly sterilizing aboriginal, black and disabled women. Abortion on demand did not always deliver *them* reproductive freedom. Nearly twenty years after mistaking their experiences for everyone else's, white, able-bodied feminists listened to the voices of these more marginalized women and redefined choice to account for other realities. The promise of belonging followed that border opening.

But the promise has not been fulfilled, not by a long shot. The nagging concern about feminism mirrors that about democracy itself: Have its borders become so flexible that anything goes, or have they remained so rigid that the message of equality rings hollow, ensuring alienation either way? Who does the mainstream really represent?

Former *Toronto Star* columnist Donna Laframboise claims that feminism's "lunatic fringe" has gone mainstream. Taking cues from dissident American feminists such as Camille Paglia and Katie Roiphe, Laframboise's 1996 book *The Princess at the Window* attempts a Canadian spin on the controversy. Women of colour, our movement's relative rookies, she says, have seized the reins and made racism such a central issue that more relevant issues are getting squeezed out. On behalf of white women, Laframboise assures that "many of us didn't mind emphasizing race for a while. But we've grown tired of being told not only that we oppress our sisters but that we haven't shown any willingness to share power." Prompted by such supposed extremism, Laframboise seeks to "intercept the pendulum … before it reaches the outer limits and then slices through all of us on the rebound."

Another damsel in dissent, Oregon journalist Rene Denfeld, deems middle-aged feminists the "New Victorians"—a prudish lot with a patronizing insistence on a morality of Birkenstocks, vegetarianism, goddess worship and sexual repression. Like Victorian women, Denfeld writes, contemporary feminists have excused themselves from the sphere of real action, pronounced themselves dainty divas and left young women with no mainstream movement to join.

Similarly, Clark University philosophy professor Christina Hoff Sommers calls herself a "feminist who doesn't like what feminism has become." What feminism has become, we are told, is a hysterical socialist demand that society's institutions change to suit women—a violation, she suggests, of feminism's original goal that women be given the opportunity to adapt to society's institutions. Moderate "equity feminism" has been hijacked by a left-wing "gender feminism." So Hoff Sommers answers the question bellowed by her book's title, *Who Stole Feminism?* Her premise, reinforced by Laframboise, is that somebody owns feminism.

Which brings me to Susan Faludi, author of the 1991 best-seller *Backlash*. While eerily echoing the dissidents' premise of ownership, in a 1995 *Ms.* magazine article she dismisses them as "Pod Feminists," aliens who have teamed up with the right-wing media to invade, then abduct, the "body of the women's movement." Only sentences later, Faludi brands the dissidents "faux feminists," or imitations of the real thing.

Hardly a pillow fight, the barrage of labels does not encourage me to look for belonging from North America's feminist divas. Still, like the kid who pawned homemade lunches to boost interaction with her classmates, I call myself a feminist because I believe the movement and the society with which it bargains have the potential to accept me just enough to explore my reality further.

It would seem that society already has. The immigration officer gave me hope as a child. Twenty-five years later, who would dispute that I have enjoyed some career opportunities because I am different and it is time for another perspective? Yet these are superficial markers of belonging. I am willing to wear labels, including "feminist," "woman of colour" and "Muslim lesbian," as an entrée into conversation. But that conversation must take place. Otherwise the labels stick, get confused with an identity and frustrate belonging.

The clamping of communication can happen with incredible subtlety and in the most unlikely of places.

CHAPTER 2

the b.s. of breakthroughs

"Irshad, you have to remember that what's history to you is memory to us." That sermon, ritually delivered with a smile, rings in my head as I reflect on my short-lived breakthrough in 1992 as the first woman of colour to join the editorial board of a major Canadian newspaper. The paper was the *Ottawa Citizen*.

Those words, and similar sentiments, were meant to pooh-pooh my participation, to retire me to my playpen and to remind me that none of my ideas could compete with the expertise that the old boys had built up over the years. No doubt, at age twenty-four I had a lot to learn about journalism and life. I still do. But, brimming with experiences that my male colleagues did not share, I had a lot to contribute, too. I thought the hiring committee, which included my future boss, agreed; why else would I have been selected to help craft the official opinions of the pre-eminent newspaper in Canada's capital?

That said, I was not born yesterday. I knew full well that I had entered the newspaper's offices as the aggregate of my labels. One editorial board member joked to another about me, "She checks off all the boxes, doesn't she?" Because I was a label on legs, this breakthrough provided my first adult test of belonging. And I resolved to meet my part of the bargain by ferreting out opportunities to interact.

After completing my first week on the job, I asked my boss for feedback. "Feedback?! Feedback?! We don't do that kind of thing around here," he barked. Sometimes, interaction required risk. During one board meeting, I locked horns with the *Citizen*'s publisher, who advocated axing the country's deficit—and fast. Not at the expense of the unemployed, I piped up.

His eyes fixed on mine, the veteran journalist snapped, "Look, young lady, I'm saying this so people like you will have a future."

"People like me need a present before we can have a future," I retorted. I might have thrown a "gramps" in there for good measure. No wallflower was this young lady.

Months later, a colleague whose desk sat en route to the boardroom told me that I trooped eagerly into the morning meetings, then emerged "looking more and more weary. I couldn't imagine what happened to you in there," she confessed. War, really, and few allies. Then again, that is to be expected—another news day, another editorial board debate.

What I did not bargain for were the other battles: the periodic comments from superiors that I should dress more delicately, and the instructions I received not to dispute the biases of older journalists. In the ladies' room, I got plenty of pep talks from female reporters; in the open, where their support really mattered, they kept to themselves. As journalists, they all purported to be on the front line of free expression, yet the women could not speak out and the men would not tolerate having their assumptions questioned, least of all by a label like me. Prohibited as an editorialist from joining the union, I often felt alone in my post-breakthrough battles.

A few months after starting, I agreed, at my boss's urging, to leave. Despite my request for more time, he opined that time would do no good. It seems that I had not shown an unalloyed willingness to honour, obey and cherish his approach. Journalism, he concluded, could not be my calling.

While my breakthrough was ending, another woman's was picking up speed. In the spring of 1993, Kim Campbell uncorked her bid for the leadership of Canada's governing party, the venerable Progressive Conservatives. Although a relative neophyte in that party, she had an established presence in Canadian conservative politics. A lawyer, ex-school board trustee and one-time aide to former B.C. Social Credit premier Bill Bennett, Campbell was elected to the province's legislature in 1986. As the only self-declared "pro-choice" member of Premier Bill Vander Zalm's caucus, she became the first to break ranks when the charming, ultraconservative Vander Zalm unilaterally undertook to end provincial funding for most abortions. (The B.C. Supreme Court swiftly ruled his policy illegal.) In between, Campbell ran for the Social Credit leadership, finishing a distant last but titillating political watchers with her table-turning, anti-Zalm barb, "[C]harisma without substance is a dangerous thing."

In 1988, Campbell entered the federal House of Commons as the Tory MP for Vancouver Centre, territory held provincially at the time by prominent New Democrats. Her feisty defence of that election's defining issue, free trade, coupled with her burgeoning persona as the sharp-witted gal from the West, marked Campbell as cabinet material. Prime Minister Brian Mulroney soon moved her there, initially as a junior minister for Indian affairs, then as head of the heavy justice and defence portfolios. At Justice, Campbell radiated fearlessness. By the time Mulroney announced his resignation in February 1993, all eyes had turned to the woman who made even judges' robes look risqué.

If hers was a fairytale rise up the Tory pole, party brass did not caution Campbell to keep her expectations realistic. Just the opposite: senior male politicians deferred to her poll numbers and dropped out of the running. One cited an "unprecedented consensus" that Campbell, then Canada's first female defence minister, would become Canada's first female prime minister. Four months later, groomed but doomed, she reached the Conservative throne and the prime minister's office.

Four months after that, in a nationwide election, Campbell oversaw the most resounding defeat of the Conservatives in Canadian history. Her government was gone, her party in tatters, her career in free-fall. About her summer at the top, Campbell told Newsworld host Anne Petrie, "I felt [that] in many ways, who I was and what I stood for kind of got lost ... There is a temptation to see women, particularly, as one-dimensional, and none of us is one-dimensional."

But the precedent of the breakthrough remained, and for journalist Margaret Wente, it was the breakthrough, not the follow-through, that held weight. "The women have at last arrived, not as token but as equal players in national political life," gushed the editor of the Globe and Mail's "Report on Business" magazine. She later dripped with delight at the appointment of Maureen Kempston Darkes to steer General Motors Canada, among the country's largest companies. "Women at the top are so rare that every addition to the tiny club of CEOs is a major breakthrough," Wente enthused. The title of her column: "Women in power, and the paths they took."

Her euphoric premise that the simple act of breaking through signals a balance of power is the delirium inflicted by what I term the Break-through Syndrome. B.S. patients exhibit a myopia that is at once soothing and dangerous. Like those who will not lift up labels, sufferers of B.S. do not bother peering past the breakthrough to probe what happens next and why. Rather, they assume that as soon as a woman pierces the glass ceiling of a nontraditional field, she has "made it." These delusions lead B.S. patients to believe that how a woman fares after her breakthrough depends entirely on her own merits. In turn, that belief props up politically charged distortions of employment equity, feeding stereotypes of who deserves a good job and who does not.

Symptoms of the syndrome can also be traced in recent books by dissident feminists. Kate Fillion's 1996 best-seller, *Lip Service*, argues that despite having other ways to impress the boss, many young women (of the primarily white, middle-class, heterosexual sample she surveyed) choose to seduce him. Lust, aggression, competition and poor judgement can thus accompany female power just as often they do male authority. Similarly, in *The Princess at the Window*, Donna Laframboise writes that by broadening the definition of discomfort, many workplace harassment policies sap women's power and men's dignity, ultimately undermining our common humanity.

While I do not downplay the human temptation to abuse power, both authors—along with Margaret Wente—presume the equal power of career women to be a fact. In effect, B.S. patients reduce the Kim Campbells of our world to an unexplored label: "equal players," in Wente's words.

The best remedy for B.S. is a reality check, downed with a dose of vigilance. If power is the ability to produce the intended result, as British philosopher Bertrand Russell suggested, then snagging an eighteenth-floor office hardly levels the playing field between men and women. As long as women have to squeeze into a culture designed without them in mind, they will easily be marginalized within it.

Even at the prime ministerial echelon. "Power, as I learned that summer, is much more than holding a formal position," Campbell writes in her 1996 memoirs, *Time and Chance*. "If no one will support you, it matters little what your title is." Or what your promise is. Campbell pledged to "do politics differently," but to produce the intended result, she first had to belong. As her part of the belonging bargain, Campbell bowed to many rules of established politics. She diluted her feminism to push a bill that recriminalized abortion, pandered to mass prejudice by moving the immigration file to a newly named Ministry of Public Security and dramatized her scrappiness for the cameras throughout. Her compromises were not reciprocated.

In the November 1992 speech that set her star ablaze, Campbell shattered the silence about her "unspeakable" loneliness so close to the apex of Canadian politics. "Women's frontal lobes have always been accepted," she said about the culture of politics, "but the gender-specific aspects of our personality have not." That there are gender-specific aspects of women's personalities, I am unsure. But the point is, despite appearing to be inside the old boys' sandbox—despite being labelled an equal player—the reality of Campbell's power remained dubious.

Conspiracy aficionados suspect that Tory cronies set Campbell up for a tumble, harking back to Flora MacDonald's fishy failure to capture the Conservative Party leadership in 1976. More revealing of Campbell's power, I think, is what happened to her after the 1993 defeat. Although appointed in 1996 as Canada's counsel-general in Los Angeles, she flitted from lecturing contract to broadcasting contract for almost three years before that. Over half a century since Canada's first female member of parliament, Agnes Macphail, lost her seat and left federal politics, Campbell faced the same situation: unmarried and unapologetic, she had an uncertain financial future.

By contrast, male politicians at that level can depend on corporate directorships as post-defeat cushions. Campbell's predecessor, Brian Mulroney, secured three such seats within months of resigning as prime minister. At one point, Ontario ex-premiers David Peterson, Bill Davis and Frank Miller laid claim to thirteen, seventeen and six directorships respectively. John Turner, whose probation as prime minister ended more quickly than Campbell's, has savoured ten corporate pay cheques. On top of that, nearly all these men draw healthy pensions from their years in one parliament or another. Nearly all earn big money as part-time pooh-bahs at their law firms. Campbell enjoys neither privilege. So much for her breakthrough being a seal of equal legitimacy and a door to belonging.

In spite of our separate professions and vastly different stations on the career ladder, Campbell's post-breakthrough experiences chart much the same pattern as mine. If our aim was to improve hackneyed approaches in our lines of work, and our hope was to be appreciated for our unique perspectives, our time was spent suppressing our distinct voices. To recall Michael Ignatieff, the dominant culture did not care to look beneath our differences to forge an identity. The message of our breakthrough: Culture does not change; you do.

Until workplace culture adapts to women as much as women adapt to it, the measure of a successful breakthrough will be not meaningful participation but mere survival. And survival—on an editorial board as well as on Parliament Hill—will have harsh conditions. Longtime journalist Susan Riley, the person I replaced on the *Citizen*'s editorial board, sees two brutal ways for women to survive: Aspire to be one of the boys or prepare early to quit. Riley went a kinder, gentler third route: the back alley. "I didn't fight them [the men]," she remembers. "I tried to smuggle feminism into everything on the ed board." Yet smuggling implies a defiance of somebody else's rules. So the smuggle-to-survive strategy does not necessarily challenge an arrogant culture; it might only perpetuate the illusion of openness.

That lesson was confirmed for me by another feminist smuggler, Catherine Ford. "There are rules about corner offices," she explains, "and as long as men only want to play by those rules, women have to play by them too." As boss of the *Calgary Herald*'s editorial board for nine years, Ford gathered her male minions and few superiors around a table that she had custom-built for her office. "Rule number one: Authority is invested in territory. If you have only men above you and *your* meetings are in *their* offices and you're a woman and you're a manager, how much power do you really have? Already, you're one step behind because you're not a man, so what do you do? You have a table specially built for your office so the men understand whose meeting this is.

"I hope that one day women won't have to be as aggressive as me to be in my position," she volunteers. "Meanwhile, we're still here. Territory and toys."

In 1995, Ford stepped down as associate editor of the *Herald* to become a syndicated columnist. She cryptically confessed to a reporter that "the time had come when I had to ask myself, 'Am I happy?' "Still, she stuck it out for almost a decade because, as she earlier told me, "I want to pass a torch down to a whole generation of people who won't have to play the games I did." Logically so, except that as long as women agree to play those games for the sake of professional endurance, future generations will continue to be deemed credible by their "personality fit" with the system. Even a critical mass of women, then, might not loosen the levers of power. The public face of an institution will have changed. Its private culture will persevere.

The Breakthrough Syndrome does not affect only male-dominated environments; assumptions about the invulnerability of women who have "made it" plague feminist-driven workplaces as well. B.S. deceives feminists into believing that they are genuinely sharing power with newcomers. But the recent breakthroughs of two women of colour illustrate otherwise. Neither woman's profile pretends to be an exhaustive look at what happens in her workplace. Rather, each story is meant to examine the nuances of exclusion from one vantage point—that of the person who senses it.

In 1992, Joanne St. Lewis became the first black executive director of the Women's Legal Education and Action Fund (LEAF), a national organization of feminist lawyers who have influenced Supreme Court rulings on such issues as the rape shield law, the peddling of pornography and the taxation of child support. A fully bilingual lawyer who grew up in Quebec and Ontario, St. Lewis accepted LEAF's top post after years of high-profile advocacy: she was special advisor to the grand council of the Crees of Quebec, assistant to the head of the Ontario Human Rights Commission and a member of LEAF's own legal committee. Given that organization's stated commitment to equality, and its record of defending cases involving women with diverse realities, St. Lewis hoped to find there "a level of comfort as a minority." Instead, the new executive director got contempt for her credentials and complacency about how racism infected the workplace.

After only a year of being LEAF's public ambassador and private challenger, St. Lewis lost any delusion of comfort and any stamina to stay. Although she quit her job, she kept her sense of humour. "I think it was one of those things that your mother calls a 'growth experience,'" she laughs. "Problem was, I was a full-grown adult already and hadn't been planning on a growth experience at this time. What a bonus."

St. Lewis has long known that bitterness gets her nowhere in the search for belonging. At age nine, decked out in a dress and ribbons that her grandmother had sent from Trinidad, she found herself being chased through a Montreal-area school yard and beaten up by white teenagers. "Nobody helped me. I remember running past teachers and being in the farthest corner of the school yard and fighting back and being taken to the principal's office and not knowing what happened to these teenagers. My child's memory is that nobody intervened." For days, she "vibrated with rage, almost into my separate molecules." Then her father asked St. Lewis to articulate how she felt about her tormentors. "I said, 'They don't know me. I don't know them. And they hurt me. I hate them.' " Her father pointed out that her reaction "might just be the most important thing in my life, because if I didn't find a way to manage my anger, it was going to end up being the centre of my world.

"For me, that's a pivotal memory of trying to deal with the fact that people could really hurt me, just because I was different. I realized that while I couldn't always control what happens to me, I can control my response to it. It's a lesson I've brought to all the work I do."

Including her work in supposedly feminist surroundings. If nobody stood up for the black child in the school yard, neither did "actual knowledge of racism" within LEAF produce what St. Lewis needed: "a concerted organizational voice saying, 'This is unacceptable. We have a set of principles by which we're guided. We're going to address this thing.' "

During her inaugural week, St. Lewis had to fight to have the principles of employment equity followed in hiring an office fund-raiser. Despite LEAF's professed support of equity policies, no minority individual had been interviewed for the position by the time St. Lewis arrived. "This was like the slippery slope to hell for me," St. Lewis says. "I'm on my fourth day of work, and I'm now sitting in a meeting with people I don't know. Do I remind them of their commitment? Do I question their hiring practices? Do I remain silent? If I remain silent, I can't reassure myself that they actually had a qualified pool and settled on candidates through a process I can justify. I'm their new administrative head, I'm a woman of colour, and I'm going to have to defend all of this in public. How could I possibly justify this given the politics I espouse? I was damned if I did and damned if I didn't."

So she did. Given that some staff thought the fund-raising job an affirmative action position, the new executive director sought clarification from a board member. According to St. Lewis, the board member said, "If there was a single woman of colour capable of writing a proper grant application, I would know of her. Since I don't know of her, she doesn't exist. You're wasting my time, you're wasting the organization's time."

St. Lewis was stunned. "We had no personal relationship, no animosity, nothing. [Yet] this is a conversation with the volume rising at every moment. Second week of work, and she's telling my little black ass that I'm a blasted idiot for what I'm doing there."

More visible incidents of hostility did not go unnoticed by some members of LEAF, St. Lewis emphasizes. Those who saw or heard bigotry "were horrified." The problem was not the absence of a double take over racism but the presence of a double standard when reacting to it. "When feminists argue about sexism, we tend to say that the person's intention isn't relevant. If something's sexist, it's sexist. Period. So what annoyed me—and that's a minor way of putting it—was people explaining to me how poor so-and-so's social skills were or how idiosyncratic their behaviour was. But being the recipient of this behaviour, I, in my perversity, concluded that racism was alive and well and people should help me do something to uproot it." Chats with the sympathetic chairperson and the few women of colour on LEAF's board only went so far.

Nowhere did the double standard cause St. Lewis more pain than in her struggle to have LEAF respond to a racist letter from an individual member. The letter was prompted by the support St. Lewis publicly expressed for the election of Sunera Thobani, a South Asian, as president of the National Action Committee on the Status of Women. "It appears that Canadian citizenship has ceased to have any value," wrote the elderly correspondent. "The work of my white-skinned British ancestors and successive generations are to [be] sneered at and violated by dark-skinned immigrants." She added that she "used to be a feminist, but no more," concluding that the "memory of the achievements of Emily Murphy, Nellie McClung, et al., is being dragged in the gutter ... Of course, these women were citizens with Canadian experience who had served their apprenticeships." (For the record, pioneer feminist Nellie McClung might well have disassociated herself from the correspondent's remarks. Some eighty years ago, she condemned the "blind egotism" of many a white Canadian, adding admonishingly that "[w]e Anglo-Saxon people have a decided sense of our own superiority, and we feel sure that our skin is exactly the right colour ... So we naturally look down upon those who happen to be of a different race and tongue than our own.")

When St. Lewis recommended an official LEAF response to the

correspondent, "the immediate answer was that she's old, she's cranky, she didn't know what she was saying. I said no; age doesn't shield you from being racist. I don't care if you're Sophia on the [U.S. sitcom] *Golden Girls* or my own grandmother—you should be accountable for what you say and do." Eventually, LEAF published a strong denunciation of the toxic letter, but not before a dogged St. Lewis lobbied and educated.

The accumulated stress led to protracted menstual bleeding and persuaded St. Lewis to resign. She now teaches law at the University of Ottawa, making her one of Canada's few black professors. Do not automatically applaud that breakthrough, she cautions. Lift up the breakthrough and sniff inside for support. "People underestimate what it is to be a black woman and take positions of the type that I do. Often at the level, you're the only person of colour, so you're constantly having to replenish yourself—by yourself—if you face any opposition. Meanwhile, you're constantly giving out energy to others. At LEAF, I had a sense that there were people who respected my skills, but the emotional feedback I needed to replenish the energy I expended just didn't happen. I think that's partially because of this myth about black women's capacity to cope."

Indeed, during her bleeding spell, St. Lewis heard from a friend who knew two other women with a similar problem. Inquiring further, she found that "we were all women of colour in senior positions, having 'made it,' trying to transform institutions. And each of us was ill." Intellectually, she grasped this phenomenon so well that, for the sake of survival, St. Lewis implemented a Susan Riley–style lesson: prepare early for the departure. From the first month of her breakthrough, St. Lewis publicly hinted that she would not, or could not, stick around. "I remember saying at a conference in November [1992] that one of the essential problems of changing 'feminist' organizations is how women of colour get used. These organizations are transformed literally with our life blood. Their needs absorb our psychic and physical energies. The hubris on my part was thinking that I'm an unlimited source of energy, and that this was a reasonable sacrifice to make for what was at stake."

Ironically, St. Lewis's narrow choices forced her to feed the myth of boundless coping capacity. In yet another display of damned-if-you-do-and-damned-if-you-don't, her lifelong survival tool, anger management, might have served to downplay the problems. "It's really maddening that because I don't deal with things from the victim stance, people don't bother to understand how genuinely painful and destructive some environments are for me," she laments. That is why, she suspects, even allies on the LEAF board "didn't see the issues as the urgent ones I saw them as."

Commenting "factually" about racism got St. Lewis no further than if she had been emotional about it, tipping her off to the power imbalance at play. "As long as some people have to manage themselves while others have the luxury of expressing the totality of who they are, we're in a discriminatory dynamic," St. Lewis notes. It is an observation that not only calls to mind the expressive freedom of the Gen Xer compared to that of the aboriginal woman, but also speaks to the separate realities of women and men in the *Citizen* newsroom. As for being a women of colour in the LEAF office, when you are not permitted to communicate as a whole feminist in an avowedly feminist organization, you know it is not just men who power-trip. "Feminists talk as though backlash is something outside of our organizations," says St. Lewis. "But it's inside the movement too."

Sunera Thobani's post-breakthrough struggles attest to the truth of Joanne St. Lewis's statement. Between 1993 and 1996, Thobani presided over the National Action Committee on the Status of Women (NAC), one of Canada's liveliest lobby groups. She stepped aside midway into her second term.

The first woman of colour to head NAC, Thobani learned early on that many feminists expected "their" movement to crumble under her leadership. In that sense, she let them down. During the 1994 NAC convention, her first as president, she navigated the diverse delegates to common waters on an issue that threatened to sink the good ship *Solidarity*. I watched as she waited her turn at the microphone, then cautioned the convention to "be realistic." The opposition hissed. Thobani introduced a compromise. The disagreement was diluted. Finally, the voters passed her proposal. While a couple of delegates huffed out—a lower loss than in previous years—several beside me thanked the Goddess above for a president who could negotiate solutions. Earlier, Thobani had devoted a third of her keynote speech to young women. The students I sat with savoured the acknowledgement; something older feminists are not much good at giving, they said.

So where did the old girls' fear of Thobani's leadership stem from? A gap in culture, Thobani suggests. "I don't fit into the way the feminist network talks to each other—the familiarity, the friendships. These women don't relate in the same way without that cultural affinity."

Sometimes, they do not relate at all. Thobani remembers key executive members inexplicably excusing themselves from NAC's participation in the 1993 federal election campaign. Only later did they divulge the reason: they felt excluded because Thobani had not explicitly invited them to get involved, even though campaign activities were among the responsibilities for which executive members had signed up and been elected. In other words, these women did not need a direct overture; they were there for that purpose.

To be sure, "a number of white women were open to talking," but not sufficiently to stop the shrinking of Thobani to a label. At one feminist conference, the planners—ever sensitive to "inclusion"—categorized participants according to the organizations they represented. They listed Thobani under Women of Colour. "I reminded them that I'm not president of a strictly women-of-colour organization," she says curtly. "It's pointless to keep getting angry about it, but to constantly not be seen this way—you're never 'more than,' you're 'less than.' "

Even those who think they are restoring balance to feminist practice can cave to reductionist temptations. In *The Princess at the Window*, Donna Laframboise fumes that "no matter how many hours you've poured into good causes, [some feminists] feel no compunction whatever about slandering your good name on the flimsiest of grounds." That is a reference to the accusations of racism hurled by some women of colour at June Callwood, a social justice crusader and founder of Nellie's Hostel for Women in Toronto, the scene of this 1992 controversy. I share Laframboise's skepticism about the accusations, which were both confusing and confused. But two pages before, she replicates the very sin that she castigates—"slandering [a] good name on the flimsiest of grounds."

In her first mention of Thobani, Laframboise describes her simply as "a graduate student who'd been living in Canada for just four years" when she ascended to the NAC presidency. No mention of the "many hours" Thobani had already "poured into good causes": that she had been a peace activist since her college days in Britain and the U.S.; that she finished her feminist apprenticeship in Canada, sitting on the co-ordinating collective of the Vancouver Status of Women; that she chaired NAC's committees on violence against women and reproductive technologies; that in the latter role, she steeled her spine to challenge a doctor who was popular in Vancouver's South Asian community because his fertility clinic catered to couples wanting baby boys. Above all, no mention that Thobani has been credited for "the maturity of the abortion rights movement in B.C. today."

Instead, Thobani is introduced, and reduced, to a "student" who has been here for "just four years." Read: unemployed, inexperienced immigrant.

The trend of labelling Thobani, imperceptibly or brazenly, was set even before she took office. In covering her election to the presidency of NAC, the national media focussed not on her resumé, nor on her private history of juggling single motherhood and formal study, but on the words of one rarely-heard-from man. John MacDougall, a Conservative member of parliament, declared Thobani to be an "illegal" immigrant with little knowledge of Canadian women's issues. On both fronts, he misfired. MacDougall said he received his information in an unmarked envelope, but neither he, nor the media, cared to investigate further. In a news conference the next day, Thobani and her predecessor, U.S.-born Judy Rebick, set the record straight. Proven wrong yet protected by parliamentary immunity, a barely known backbencher managed to grab headlines that gave him national credibility.

A year later, and a minute's stroll from the site of MacDougall's salvo, journalists grilled Thobani in tones that suggested she should be skewered. Wasn't it just a gimmick? asked one reporter, referring to NAC's noisy but failed attempt that day to meet with the ostensibly populist Reform Party about its anti-equality policies. The NAC march ended in some scuffling with, and screaming among, Parliament's security guards. How could you possibly think it would achieve anything? wondered another reporter. You talk about the need for democracy, but where's your respect for democracy in storming Parliament? persisted a third.

"[T]here was clear disapproval in the media questions which, incidentally, all came from female journalists," noted *Citizen* columnist Susan Riley, exposing the farce of journalistic objectivity. "It was another reminder of the insular and conservative nature of Ottawa's political culture."

Riley's observation reinforced what Rosemary Speirs, as Ottawa bureau chief for the *Toronto Star*, confessed about female journalists in coveted parliamentary posts: "We're so busy playing a man's game by men's rules that we're just adding our voices to what the boys are saying [in a] culture which tends to absorb women."

As Thobani stood at the press podium defending NAC against charges of stupidity, hypocrisy and irrelevancy, it was clear that the Breakthrough Syndrome had targeted her twice. First, as long as those female reporters had to behave like men to get their stories, Thobani did not have a prayer. Her in-your-face feminism directly clashed with their on-the-job sex changes. That press conference uncovered the value of *their* breakthroughs. Second, Thobani's own breakthrough suffered from the discomfort these women felt at letting someone outside of their galaxy influence the national agenda. NAC had marched loudly on Parliament Hill more than once during Rebick's presidency. Why was the media moralizing now? In fact, many of the news items that week openly cast doubt on whether NAC represented the mainstream any more. The *Citizen*'s Janice Kennedy, an avowed feminist, pronounced hockey commentator and pucking loudmouth Don Cherry less embarrassing than "these shrill little interest groups."

The impression Kennedy left was that NAC no longer matters to anybody but immigrant lesbians with a limp and a lisp. Ironic, because in the days leading up to that march on Parliament, NAC held a convention that would have frustrated anyone on the hunt for extremism. At a workshop on lesbian issues, for instance, the majority of participants wore skirts. And as far as I could see, most had clean-shaven legs. (Research required me to look. Honest.) Two floors below, near the main entrance of the hotel ballroom, a Mary Kay cosmetic rep smiled in front of her booth. One of the conference organizers had invited her, she said. Although still awaiting that "rousing response" from delegates, she winked and grinned. "Tomorrow morning, I'll be giving two of them facials right here, just so the women walking by can see what they're missing." Dykes without ankle stubble and a make-up madame without shame at the country's fieriest feminist fest—NAC had not grown too extreme since Thobani's presidency.

Yet, from that week on, even columnists known for their effervescent compassion felt licence to distort. In an October 1994 musing about Canada's social policy debate, the *Globe and Mail*'s resident liberal, Michael Valpy, claimed that NAC "has become increasingly narrow in its representation."

Thobani grits her teeth at that quote: "I responded in a letter to the editor, which the *Globe* didn't run." In it, she pointed out that NAC's conference on social policy was not only the first such event in Canadian history to be jointly sponsored by women's groups from Quebec and the rest of the country; it was also the first nationwide challenge to the Chrétien government's unravelling of social programs. And if NAC concentrated on defending social programs in 1994, its priority campaign in 1993—tailored to the federal election—was jobs. "Who in their right mind would argue these are issues only for immigrant and racial minority women?" Thobani asks. Not anyone who has been listening to her throughout: in her first week as NAC president, the *Financial Post* queried Thobani about her thoughts on employment equity. She replied that it is an important policy for women, "but right now we see the fight has to be for jobs." A rather mainstream way of catering to special interests.

Doubtless, immigrant interest in NAC has shot up since Thobani became president—boosting, not busting, the group's constituency. Thanks to the increased demands for appearances (up to six a week in Canada), Thobani raised four times as much money as expected in her inaugural presidential year. Because of slashed government grants and an internal fund-raising fiasco in the following years, the growing audience of newcomers has played no small part in NAC's self-sufficiency. The $74,000 deficit Thobani inherited was paid down by her final year as president. Most surprising to her, however, "is all the men from immigrant communities who've turned out for our events. Now they see NAC speaking up not only for women but for people of colour, too. I think they're recognizing that the links we're making translate into a better life for entire families and communities."

Perhaps other Canadians do not know about these achievements because Thobani's accent cannot be understood—the theory politely posed to her by one female journalist. " 'If only you sounded like us, or were like us, then we wouldn't have this unease.' That's what they're saying," reckons Thobani, who has always donned her baggy, brightly embroidered Indian pantsuits as the least restrictive clothes going. Optics, along with accents, can overshadow accomplishments. They are the stuff of which labels are made. The cultural "unease" that Thobani detects among many female journalists retraces the "cultural affinity" that she sees exercised by many feminist activists.

Now for the good news: Thobani has also seen moments that suggest the old girls' network is opening up. This is how she sustained her breakthrough and why she stood for a second term as NAC president. After months of wanting to get out while the getting, and her health, were good, Thobani reconsidered when women in the union movement, latching onto the concerns of many women of colour, made a last-ditch appeal. Serve again, said the labour feminists, and we will help raise money for NAC every year. To flesh out that support, labour ran one of its own for the vice-presidency—a gesture of cooperation unheard of during Thobani's first term. She emphasizes cooperation when clarifying her decision to stay on. "Women of colour were pressing me to remain because, however hard it had been for me, an important milestone was reached. We could not lose this chance to consolidate our gains and move ahead. Also, labour women feared that the bridges built between various communities and causes during my presidency would be washed away if I went at [that] time."

Such worries might have been warranted. In 1996, the Canadian Labour Congress and NAC organized a cross-country women's march against poverty—the biggest show of women in national history to address a problem that haunts Canadian families. Over the month-long life of the march, more than 100,000 women physically participated. The final event, a demonstration on Parliament Hill, put a lie to the assumption that diversity must equal disunity. "The leadership of women of colour and aboriginal women was completely visible," Thobani asserts, adding that women with disabilities also made their presence known. NAC now has a disability rights committee.

The women's march against poverty marked Thobani's last commitment as NAC president. She resigned in June 1996, explaining that she wants to spend more time with her growing daughter and that her goals of accountability, representation and financial sustainability had been achieved. The new president, women's health advocate Joan Grant-Cummings, promises to continue reaching out, especially to northern, rural and younger women.

That Thobani hung in where St. Lewis packed it in is not puzzling. Thobani's greater visibility meant more responsibilities to others and, therefore, a different perception of the stakes involved. St. Lewis considered the price of staying too high for her health; Thobani figured that, the personal toll aside, exiting after one term would jeopardize the deepening of NAC's relationship with women of colour—a damning prospect for a grassroots feminist organization.

Equally decisive was the difference between their circles of support. Truly lonely at the top, St. Lewis almost always had to energize herself. Not so at NAC. Although neither white women nor women of colour form a united front, enough embraced Thobani to back her hopes for a less racist organization.

These hopes are why, despite facing cries of reverse racism, Thobani publicly stated that a woman of colour should succeed her. Wrote Thobani in the *Toronto Star*, "The strongest commitment by white women to anti-racism will be meaningless if they are unable to actually work with women of color on a basis of equality. Electing a woman of color president is one thing, but making sure she then has the cooperation and support necessary to fulfill her responsibilities is quite another. Until women of color can be accepted as equals, it is important that a woman of color lead NAC." For all their differences, Sunera Thobani, Catherine Ford, Joanne St. Lewis and Kim Campbell have found common ground in discussing the lack of post-breakthrough support.

If the future of policies like employment equity looks dire, it is not just because of narrow neo-conservative politicians. It is also because good old-fashioned liberals, including self-described feminists, fail to grasp that breakthrough women amount to tired tokens when they cannot challenge anything more than the complexion of institutions. In employment equity, as in all efforts to belong, support is key. Support dismantles barriers between people and jobs, people and people, people and social change. Until that is realized, the Breakthrough Syndrome will spread, convincing the afflicted that all we need for belonging are more individual precedents. In reality, we need a culture of interaction.

Sunera Thobani does believe that white women can fight racism. As she asked *Star* readers, "What on earth would I be doing inside NAC if I believed [otherwise]?" Thobani later told me, "You get involved and help transform the mainstream or you become a separatist. For me, separatism is not an option." Carved from a suburb of Toronto, "an independent South Asian Republic of Scarborough," she said half-jokingly, "won't solve anything."

But for many people, separatism is not only an option; it is the best one. Scarcely the sole preserve of biological determinists, the practice of "identity politics" can be found among the least usual suspects. This postmodern craze has "common sense" roots, touching the proverbial White Straight Man no less than the Muslim Lesbian Feminist.

CHAPTER 3

identity politics:
the common sense evolution

My recovery from the Breakthrough Syndrome has taught me that systemic discrimination wears two faces today—one obvious, one obscure. Time was when its face was only obvious. You would have to be white and male to take your seat in a certain workplace. That is not always true now; you can be a "young lady" and sit with the big boys on an editorial board. The catch is, you are required to emulate the dominant culture.

Since childhood, I have known that belonging takes some bending. As an adult, I have learned that the power lies with those who decide how much you must bend before you are allowed to belong. You can bend until you are blue in the face, but without recognition of your efforts—without the right to belong—you will continue to be a label; more so if you "check off all the boxes."

In contemporary parlance, this reduction of individuals to aspects of their physical portfolios is called "identity politics." It is the belief that any one of our biological dimensions—sex, colour, ethnicity, (dis)ability, sexual orientation, age—and, by extension, class and religion, provide a sufficiently solid foundation on which to form a community. More than fostering community, identity politicians often attempt to secure a political advantage for that trait which distinguishes their community. Beware the implications for democracy.

In its benign stage, identity politics can help us see through the platitude that ours is a meritocracy which rewards individuals for who they are and what they have achieved, not for who they know and what they have inherited, be it money, genitals or pigmentation. My cautionary tales of breakthrough women highlight the hollowness of that platitude. But being double-edged, identity politics too readily sweeps the unique truths about each of us under racial, sexual, economic and other generalizations. When that occurs, our individual dispositions and contradictions are obliterated for the sake of collective coherence. Ethnic cleansing anyone? Much of the world wades in the blood sucked by those who decree that individuals can have only one defining identity, a single space to which they must remain loyal or be cast out as traitors when lucky, corpses when not.

Although Canada is nowhere near Croatia (geographically or politically), our identity politicians sometimes raise the spectre of the Balkan minefield. Quebec sovereigntists paint their nationalism as strictly territorial, but by denying aboriginal people their own hopes for territorial independence—by insisting that First Nations be part of the same political state as the French-speaking nation—Quebec sovereigntists are actually asserting the dominance of one ethnicity over another. Affirms York University professor Reg Whitaker in the 1996 anthology *Clash of Identities*, "[t]he sovereigntist claim is, at root, ethnic ...

> It is driven by identity politics, and that identity is not with the abstract construct of a territory or a provincial government jurisdiction, but with a 'people,' an ethnic linguistic majority with a particular historical experience, a shared sense of collective grievance and an aspiration toward a collective historical destiny. The refusal of the minorities and the aboriginal peoples to join in the 'territorial' project puts paid to the viability of territorial sovereignty, at least on its own rhetorical terms.

Whether it happens murderously or just militantly, whether practised by Quebec sovereigntists or by advocates of aboriginal self-government, when the externalities of our nations masquerade as windows into our individual souls, we are simplified. We are run through a strainer of assumptions and reduced to a bland purée. In that context, identity politics might be better termed the "Moulinex Reflex." This near-mechanical impulse to dice, slice and chop human beings into easily digestible quarters, or blend them into a uniform pulp, removes the choices to refine our perceptions of ourselves and others, which are the crux of belonging. At its democratic best, the Moulinex Reflex lets us choose which label we would prefer to be preserved in—not whether we would prefer to be bottled into one at all.

Thus, I sympathize when John Fekete assails identity politics as a "new primitivism." The Trent University professor, a former social activist, has no time for women-of-colour caucuses and aboriginal assemblies because, he argues, identity politics "has no time for humankind." But Fekete should frown as fiercely on the primitivism to which women of colour and aboriginal people are responding—the not-so-new racism and sexism that Sunera Thobani rightly refers to as "cultural affinity." Throughout his searing 1994 polemic *Moral Panic*, Fekete presumes that the only folks who play identity politics are the self-confessed oppressed: women, natives, people of colour, gays and lesbians, the poor, the disabled; in short, the captives of an overt groupthink. He fails to see that those who enforce "common sense" can be equally big on group bonds and biological one-upmanship. An example of common sense as groupthink is the pressure put on Catherine Ford, Kim Campbell and female reporters in the parliamentary press gallery to "think male" when they broke into positions traditionally held by men. Of course, these women did not receive a memo from on high instructing them to "be men"; the conventional wisdom, or common sense, of the workplace culture conveyed that message adequately.

Other illustrations abound of the union between "common sense" and identity politics. In their 1996 best-seller *Boom, Bust & Echo*, demographer David Foot and journalist Daniel Stoffman insist that age and population trends can explain two-thirds of everything. "Most of us think of ourselves as individuals and underestimate how much we have in common with fellow members of our cohort," they write in the introduction. Later, they reassure that "for your own peace of mind, you need to understand that some of the setbacks you have experienced may relate more to demographics than to any personal failings." Having informed us that we are not merely individuals but part of an identifiable group, the authors link our privilege, or lack of it, to the status of our group. Their book is supposed make such common sense that according to its subtitle—*How To Profit from the Coming Demographic Shift*—there is serious cash in the inevitability of identity politics!

Dissident feminist Kate Fillion has also indulged in identity politics.

When H. S. Bhabra, a host of the TVOntario book show *Imprint*, asked Fillion why she restricted herself almost solely to studying the lives of white, well-educated, middle-class women for her book *Lip Service*, she said that was the group about whom she "felt qualified to make some generalizations. I hope that someone else will pursue and show how blacks and lesbians and all kinds of other women's experiences compare." Seems fair and self-restrained. After all, had Fillion's survey covered Filipino high-school drop-outs, many feminists of colour would sniff that she is "appropriating" the voices of those she cannot understand. They would not necessarily be right. Tellingly, though, Fillion's dissident feminism does not dissent with their logic. Her reply to Bhabra rehashed the identity politics line that we can comprehend only people such as ourselves. Indeed, wondered Bhabra, "Why isn't the book just called something like *Girls Like Me?*"

Even George Bush has invoked identity politics as an excuse to avoid action. After a 1992 tour of the charred, riot-ridden neighbourhoods of South Central Los Angeles, the U.S. president drawled, "I can hardly imagine the fear and the anger that people must feel to terrorize one another and burn each other's property." With Bush's Ivy League background, it is "common sense" that he would have a hard time relating. Who could blame him for pleading utter bewilderment? Edward Tivnan for one. In his 1995 book *The Moral Imagination*, Tivnan retorts:

> It is not surprising that a 68-year-old Connecticut-born son of a U.S. senator and an alumnus of Andover, Yale, the U.S. Congress, and the Central Intelligence Agency cannot put himself in the sneakers of a looter ... Yet any leader who claims, as ours so often do, to be committed to wiping out moral ugliness had better try, for while it may not be right to terrorize one another or burn one another's property, it is crucial—especially for presidents—to understand the urge.

Bush's native affiliation with particular groups of people stunted his vision of what he can, and should, attempt. His was the unspoken deployment of identity politics.

Let us be honest, then: Identity politics is like sex. Everybody does it. So what is responsible and what is reckless?

What is responsible is exercising identity politics not as an end in itself but as a means to integrity. Marshalled that way, identity politics lets us deeply examine all facets of our being—and consciously accept conflict among those facets. Consider religion. Is there anything more apparently conflictual than observing Islam and practising lesbianism at the same time? A few years ago, I could not bring myself to juxtapose those elements of my life. To try, I assumed, was to be severely deluded about the flexibility of faith. Then I met Omar. Co-founder of Salaam [Peace], an underground group of lesbian, gay and bisexual Muslims, he persuaded me that denying my dykehood might be blasphemy. Omar reminded me of Islam's noble tradition of self-inquiry—the duty to mature into faith by constantly revealing yourself to your Creator. His words recalled those of the Persian philosopher Beyazid Bestami: "For years I sought God and found myself / Now that I seek myself, I find God." Eventually, a Muslim lesbian was born.

Identity politics? No more so than the conventional politics that Salaam challenges. Its members seek love and lucidity of themselves, less a private task than a political one because we are caught between a religious leadership that rejects any harmony between homosexuality and Islam, and Western governments that tolerate homosexuality almost as well as they tolerate Islam. It is difficult to say which intolerance hurts more. It is also futile. Islam's sacred text, the Qur'an, suggests that the richness of our humanity is realized only on a lifelong migration. To fear new stations is to fear our own shadows. As one young Salaam member shrugs, "If being gay and Muslim is a contradiction, I can live with that. Contradiction is human, so I don't think in absolutes."

But there is a glitch: a lot of his, and my, detractors do think in absolutes. He and I can resolve not to drown ourselves in simplicities, yet, in a climate of profligate labelling, our discretion will not ensure reciprocity from those inclined to view us as cardboard cutouts.

Between 1994 and 1996, I engaged in weekly televised debates with conservative radio show host and author Michael Coren, himself a stout believer in defining oneself by "tribe." During the first year of our on-air sparrings, the vastly different viewer responses he and I got taught me that identity politics is often conducted by the very viewers who have the luxury to denounce it. I also learned that the responsibility I feel to exercise caution is not always met in kind.

Comments about Coren had a polite, sometimes apologetic tone. To be sure, one viewer characterized him as "that bumptious, bloated dirigible of gaseous inanity, that simpering tub of received opinion." Highly personal stuff. But rants against him were exactly that—against him, not against "his people." By contrast, peeved viewers attacked what they perceived me to represent—all uppity immigrants. If I fall into that category then so does Coren, an unretiring British chap who has lived in Canada fifteen fewer years than I. Some of our debates even stressed that fact. Curiously, when choosing between him and me, the anti-immigrant letters never mentioned him.

Rather, they served up observations such as:

> That Manji woman couldn't help herself. Arrogant immigrants are being more and more vociferously noticeable. That is why a NON-CANADIAN like Sunera Thobani has clawed her way to the top of the National Action Committee on the Status of Women. (Emphasis in original.)

The e-mail went on to vaunt "White Western cultural superiority." This, too, from a handwritten letter:

> I was appalled to tune in to hear that Muslim Woman, who professes to be Canadian, who has come to a Judeo-Christian Country and she immediately proceeds to change *us* … I welcome some immigration but I think we have gone very, very wrong in our country in this respect. My people came to Canada beginning in the 1600s from Ireland. They must be spinning in their graves at what has been done to their country! I know I *am* appalled. Multiculturalism is an abomination. (Emphasis in original.)

And this Internet message from a self-proclaimed Greek immigrant:

> What do Canadians get as a result of being so hospitable? A guest coming here and trashing the country's traditions under the umbrella of "The Charter of Human Rights" in a very unmannered way … Canada was not a deserted, not-populated land when the newcomers came. There were long-established traditions and rules

here, therefore there is no need for anyone to create/change anything.

Aboriginal nationalists might thank him for making their point nicely.

Many viewers wrote to support, sometimes laud, my arguments, especially in the second season. However, none commented on "immigrants in general," "all minorities" or "her people" after watching me. Only my critics did that. And the more they reduced me to the mascot of this or that group, the more they fuelled my need to reassert my many other selves. As such, identity politics can be necessary in answer to irresponsible reductionism.

Further, not only does one form of identity politics (racism) beget another; it often begets a more activist sort. Joanne St. Lewis explains why. "I live in a world where who I am can't be fully realized because of limitations in other people's minds," says the former executive director of LEAF.

> My job—which I didn't ask for, more like I was conscripted for—has been to find a way of making my world work properly. So where some might see activism as a little hobby, I, a black woman, don't have that choice. Either I have to twist my psyche and deny the reality of racism, or it's there anyway. And then I have to choose to let it wear me down, as if I'm washed up against the rocks at the bottom of the ocean cliff, or I have to choose to be an actor in my own life. Activism says to me: If the world is screwed up, you can manage to create spaces that function better for you; function better for people like you.

Just as St. Lewis has spent her life refusing to play a stereotype, so she resists being pummelled into passivity. That is a responsible use of identity politics, "unmannered" though it may appear to conservatives. Manners like theirs lead to manners like hers.

A pox on both houses, some might blurt; why not rise above all the teeth-gnashing with a stiff upper lip? A friend once posed that question to me, invoking my mother as an example of a "dignified" woman who never "stooped" to the gambits of her domestic and workplace tormentors. My friend misses the point of responsible activism. It is true that Mum laughed when her boss dubbed her a "spear chucker." She kept dinner warm for Dad no matter how much violence or silence he imposed on her. She got through and, yes, even grew. But like St. Lewis's anger management, which hid the reality of her pain at LEAF, Mum's stoicism alerted neither man to the agony that his identity politics was inflicting on her. The hurt she is confronting now, many years later, attests to her oppression by people who manipulated their gender and colour as reservoirs of power over her. By definition, identity politics can go away only when sexism, racism and similar abuses of power go too.

Apply that principle to the caustic viewer mail I received, and we begin to see the reckless use of identity politics. Those letters contain proof of how norms can erase responsibility. When you have bought enough into the norm of white superiority, it is never what you say or do that stokes racial division. Your norm is "common sense." It is the *resistance* to your norm that is interpreted as divisive. You are not racist; the other is.

Identity politics can be similarly mistreated by feminists, as the stories of St. Lewis and Thobani indicate. While resenting the norm-setting power of "malestream" society, many feminist communities create their own iron-clad norms and expect aspiring entrants to meet them as a condition of acceptance. Although these nontraditionalists despise the patriarchy, they pay homage to it by constituting a women's auxiliary—the Pink Patriarchy. That is, I know straight women who label themselves "lesbians" because they need an in, a base of credibility, with certain feminist coteries. Being sexually suspect, "breeders" (as straight women often get tagged) are sometimes interrogated about their politics. More commonly, from my observations, they are assumed to be lost causes, so few feminists care enough to engage them. Wearing the label "lesbian" becomes a way to avoid persecution or invisibility. Consequently, the movement is "purified" by lies. All this, in the name of power-sharing.

The challenge of making identity politics responsible rests as much with feminists as with our opponents. "I'll speak quite frankly about this because I think it's an issue feminists have to face," Thobani states.

> When I became president [of NAC], some women of colour said, "Okay, you've just joined the white girls. Essentially, you've sold out and that's how you got this position." So on the one hand you hear it from the women of colour. On the other hand, you hear

white women say, "Okay, now it's only issues of immigrants and refugees that will be addressed." And they back away.

Instead of placating one or the other set, Thobani calls for the hidden hierarchies to be "transformed into honest and visible alliances between white women and women of colour." She adds that in order to know when authoritativeness degenerates into authoritarianism, we need to recognize privilege not just in society but also in ourselves as women.

Thobani raises a crucial point. The paradox of feminist practice— shitting on each other in the guise of sharing power with each other—does not unfold in some splendid isolation. The Pink Patriarchy reflects and cements forces of hierarchy that already exist in society. Being eminently human, feminists are not immune to these forces. What *are* the forces behind identity politics?

Many chalk up identity politics to the force of post-modernism, a paradigm refined in the 1960s by French deconstructionists Jacques Derrida and Michel Foucault. Post-modernism suggests that there are no ideal truths, no unifying institutions, no objective standards, and that, therefore, everything can and should be picked apart—deconstructed—in the ceaseless search for meaning. By challenging Western philosophy's age-old way of ordering the universe, the theories of Derrida and Foucault exude revolutionary fizz.

Enter the eruption of identity politics. In his 1995 book *Nationalism without Walls*, journalist Richard Gwyn writes that Marxist ideology, having utterly failed to turn North America's crank in the sixties and seventies, has been shoved aside by the "revolutionary consciousness" of post-modernism. Like Marxists, "[p]ost-modernists are deeply concerned with the 'structures of oppression' ... especially as they bear down on identity minorities of women, gays and lesbians, and ethnic and racial groups." So much influence has the post-modern paradigm wielded that, Gwyn posits, "[t]he phrase English Canada has become politically incorrect." His is an exaggeration daily deflated by the language of news reports.

But Gwyn hints at an interesting explanation of why English Canadians, once secure and still dominant, are now "starting to think of themselves as one more multicultural group." Identity politics—whether that of elderly Quebec nationalists who do not give a damn about "English-

Canadian achievements in the two world wars" or that of young feminists of colour who condemn "patriarchal Eurocentric wisdom"—is squelching English-Canadian history. Combine the resulting loss of self-esteem with the introduction of such post-modern policies as vigorous immigration, multiculturalism and employment equity, and, Gwyn asserts, it is under- standable that "[q]uite a few [English-Canadians] have acquired the lost look of a tribe who fear they are becoming strangers in their own land." The post-modern search for meaning, then, has really meant the crass par- tition of society into colour- and gender-conscious cliques, Gwyn gripes.

They might be more crass—more aware of colour and gender—but Gwyn has not convinced me that these *conscious* cliques unleash a greater menace to social harmony than the "common sense" cliques whose *uncon- scious* practice of racism, sexism and other grades of identity politics has long helped to fragment society. Perhaps the post-modern paradigm lends legitimacy to colour- and gender-led outlooks. But create them it did not. The origins of identity politics reside in a more traditional paradigm.

Canadian communications prophet Marshall McLuhan described "a culture like ours" as being "long accustomed to splitting and dividing things as a means of control."Typically, he was onto something. For thou- sands of years, westerners have lived in cultures that encourage us to com- pete for illusions of superiority. Feeling superior implies treating someone else as inferior which, in turn, implies control of one by the other. Gener- ally known as dualism, this either/or value scheme "is the central ideolog- ical component of all systems of domination in Western society," writes U.S. social critic bell hooks.The philosophical tradition of dualism, which predates scholars as ancient as Socrates, classifies the world into oppo- sites: nature/culture, presence/absence, being/nothingness, truth/false- hood, light/darkness, man/woman. Moreover, the first element in each dichotomy has been exalted as purer, better, than the second.

These categories being western history's "common sense," aspects of our complicated human compositions are similarly fissured and pre- sumed to be irreconcilable. "As a black woman interested in [the] femi- nist movement, I am often asked whether being black is more important than being a woman; whether feminist struggle to end sexist oppression is more important than the struggle to end racism and vice-versa," hooks reports in her 1984 ground-breaker *Feminist Theory:From Margin to Center*. "All such questions are rooted in competitive either/or thinking, the belief that the self is formed in opposition to an other." hooks echoes St. Lewis and Thobani by insinuating that some of the most radical feminists stumble into dualism's arms, slapping their so-called sisters with a you-are-either-with-us-or-against-us ultimatum. Calling these women the Pink Patriarchy, as I have, implies that patriarchy itself is a product of dualism's either/or value scheme. I believe that is the case.

Broadly speaking, patriarchy is a culture of privilege based on gender that allows men in general to brandish power over women in general. That is not to say a matriarchy would be any kinder. Had women inherited most of humanity's privileges generation after generation, I doubt that history (excuse me, herstory) would be any less bruised by discrimination. Power hoarded is power abused, whoever does the hoarding. Nor is patriarchy as open as a conspiracy. Forget any diabolical plot hatched by a posse of dastardly men in a cemetery at midnight; what perpetuates patriarchy is the "common sense" assumption, made by women as well as men, that the norms we are expected to absorb are natural rather than constructed. Finally, patriarchy does not oppress all women all of the time. As Caroline Ramazanoglu admits in her 1989 book *Feminism and the Contradictions of Oppression*, many women "consent to marry men, indeed are eager to do so, and to some extent have their interests met within marriage. They can gain fulfillment as mothers, considerable control over children and the domestic economy, and an assured position in society as married women ... Patriarchy need not, then, be a wholly negative experience for women." But, she continues, "by standing back and seeing how the whole system works," we can pinpoint patriarchy's quiet power to keep countless women in their proverbial place.

The Breakthrough Syndrome, for example, feeds on that power imbalance. Mere acts of breakthrough, such as former prime minister Kim Campbell's, are insufficient to change the culture of patriarchy, because survival usually requires adherence to the either/or mentality of that culture: either I play up my scrappiness or I lose votes, either I water down my feminism or I will not be promoted within cabinet, either I accept just about every rule of the game or I start packing my bags. The cost of courting patriarchy—be it the pink or the classic brand—is an erosion of individual authenticity.

Those who accept that there is a patriarchy but doubt the depth of its power might contend that Campbell authored her own inauthenticity and subsequent misfortune by shoe-horning herself into a manmade culture. If she had displayed the fortitude to stay genuine to the "gender-specific aspects of [her] personality," the words Campbell used in her famous 1992 speech, then she would have gone further. Voters, after all, crave authenticity. What, though, would these critics tell former New Democratic Party leader Audrey McLaughlin? Another female first, she was a steadfast feminist in public and paid the price of invisibility in the media. Mainstream journalists, who also operate in an either/or value paradigm, consistently wrote off McLaughlin's trash-the-flash style as uninspiring—except when Reform Party leader Preston Manning adopted it. "As Mr. Manning rose through the right-wing ranks," McLaughlin sighs, "many of the things he was praised for were the things I was criticized for: speaking in normal tones, not pounding desks and so on. It's a no-win situation for women."

An epidemic of the Breakthrough Syndrome ensured that whatever happened to McLaughlin and Campbell after they became party leaders said more about them than about the parties they crashed. "Apologizing for women who are unpleasant and incompetent isn't going to advance the [feminist] cause," sneers political observer Heather Robertson in reference to Campbell. Agreed. I just wish that Canada's first female prime minister had been judged on her own merits; then we would know where the incompetence truly lurks—in the politician, in the patriarchy, or in both.

Internationally, the formidable power of patriarchy could be the prime reason that socialist states have failed to liberate women. Orthodox Marxists insist that the root of oppression is not patriarchy but "the exploitation of man by man on the basis of private ownership. Hence, the only way to emancipate women [is to] topple the class system." However, these Marxists warn, "as long as women are excluded from socially productive work they cannot be emancipated." That is why women must throw off the shackles of unpaid housework, or at least share those shackles with men. Only then, goes the conventional Marxist argument, will women become full partners in paid labour, political decision-making and revolutionary struggle. Scholar Maxine Molyneux says that this account of equality can be read in every official handbook on women from Vietnam to Cuba. The constitutions of these states thus contain explicit commitments to women's equality, among them the right to jobs. But the rhetoric impresses far more than the results, even in that socialist hold-out, Cuba.

Without a doubt, since Fidel Castro's collectivist coup in 1959, improved access to food, medicine, housing and schools has propelled countless Cubans towards a decent quality of life. Still, women's full inclusion in the revolution, and its benefits, has been stifled by what many acknowledge to be the persistence of machismo in Cuban society. In the early 1970s, the Federation of Cuban Women conducted a survey on why that country's government had so few female leaders. "Both male and female respondents believe … it was due to family responsibilities," the Federation found. A government study later confirmed that Cuban women did seven to fifteen times more housework than men. No wonder three-quarters of the women who joined the labour force left their jobs before a year had passed. Others settled for unpaid, voluntary work.

Taking another step in the revolutionary march, Cuba enacted the Family Code in 1975. The law assigned husbands and wives equal obligation for domestic duties, with the ultimate aim of recruiting more women to the labour force—this time for keeps. But because of the Castro government's refusal to address patriarchal biases in its economic and social practices, the Family Code did not exactly succeed. "[W]omen are hired only as needed," wrote Cuba observer Muriel Nazzari in 1983. "Linking women's job opportunities to national economic needs adds an insecurity to the lives of Cuban women that Cuban men, with guaranteed employment, do not experience."

The same stereotypes of man as breadwinner and woman as nurturer crept into Cuba's maternity law. It delivered paid leave to women before and after childbirth, but the employing enterprise had to cover those costs. As a social policy, this assumed that mothers, not both parents, must bond with newborns. Yet, as an economic policy, it did not adjust to that assumption. As a result, Nazzari concluded, "given the choice between hiring women who might become pregnant and hiring men, any enterprise required to show [productivity] would prefer to hire men." Employment statistics have corroborated her claim.

Such myopia is not unique to macho Cuba. In socialist regimes around the world, when governments have been too poor to provide the promised relief from "domestic servitude," women's equality has taken a back seat to more pressing national goals. Under socialist practice, women's liberation is negotiable, dependent upon the "national interest" as deemed by the (mostly male) powers that be. Consequently, Maxine Molyneux has noticed that "the sexual division of labour in socialist states not only bears some similarities in *form* to that prevailing under capitalism, but also in some of its *effects*." (Emphasis in original.) Caroline Ramazanoglu forthrightly sums up the global record: "More than a hundred years of socialist endeavour have produced adaptations of patriarchy rather than liberation for women." The resistance of international socialism to incorporating women as real partners in its struggle tells me that the power of patriarchy cannot be underestimated.

Those who protest that the equality of Cuban women has been hampered by that country's economic straits, exacerbated by U.S. terrorism on the trading front, make a valid point. But with or without economic growth, Castro's revolution could have, well, revolutionized portrayals of women. To a crucial degree, it did not. A symbol of the Cuban Women's Federation depicts a woman carrying a gun in one arm and a baby in the other. As Molyneux has wryly observed, "[f]ew posters of men bearing gun and infant have been sighted in the socialist countries." Rationales from endemic poverty to American imperialism ignore the fact that patriarchal prejudices are built into socialist strategy. "It is not a case of socialist states simply 'forgetting' to revolutionize relations between men and women," Molyneux argues. "On the contrary, in their official press there is quite a conscious promotion of 'motherhood' and the idea of women as naturally suited to this role because of their supposed 'spiritual, moral and physical needs.' " More than that, "[w]omen are encouraged to see themselves as having a [reproductive] responsibility" to be exercised "in accordance with wider social goals." Thus, for example, under the Sandinistas it became the patriotic duty of Nicaraguan women to produce soldiers and workers. That ostensible revolution, which took "family values" to neo-conservative peaks, kept abortion illegal. In socialist China, by contrast, women were ordered to have only one child. The legacy of China's one-child policy is a terrible new twist on women's liberation: today, any woman carrying an "unfit" foetus, as determined by the state, is "strongly encouraged" to have an abortion.

Precisely because of socialism's patriarchal impulses, New Left theory of the 1960s tacked on the "Woman Question" as if women were mere appendages to the body politic. And to many supposedly progressive men, they were. Is it any mystery why women have had to claim their integral place in North America's counterculture, never mind its mainstream culture, through what has become known as identity politics? Feminism, with its guiding principle that the personal is the political, often bears blame for being the mother of identity politics. In truth, feminism is the daughter of, and a necessary reaction to, a more powerful form of identity politics—patriarchy.

These days, though, patriarchy might be overshadowed as a force for identity politics by another manifestation of either/or values— capitalism. Laissez-faire capitalism, which now operates on a global scale, has long thrived on erecting biological categories. Hit with strikes at the Virginia coal mines, for example, nineteenth-century capitalists rushed to hire Chinese or Italian labourers. By playing the ethnic card, managers divided labourers and sapped enough energy to weaken the battle for better working conditions.

However else capitalism might be defined, its indisputable goal of maximizing profits harbours another clue that runaway capitalism entrenches divide-and-rule politics. Maximizing profits requires constant expansion. This demands colonization—an international division of labour that maintains the comfort of some at the cost of many others. But wait; we are entering the twenty-first century, when the information highway is supposed to put the brown Brazilian businesswoman on a level playing field with her white Canadian contact. So is divide-and-rule not a relic of an era when British majors-general sipped tea and supped with Indian rajas for the glory of God, Queen and Empire? The cheerleaders of globalization would like us to think so. Under laissez-faire capitalism, raves the U.S.-based WorldWatch Institute, poor countries are "growing" at rates faster than their wealthy counterparts. But to belong in the so-called global economy, many countries of the economic South have had to adopt Northern norms of progress.

The impact, as chronicled by Canadian scientist David Suzuki, starts with a narrow redefinition of human relationships:

> The International Monetary Fund/World Bank notion of development means spurning what worked in the past, ignoring the knowledge of elders and indigenous experience, and rejecting cultural

roots and tradition. It demands appraisal of everything by standards of material possession and money. A woman in Colombia told me that 20 years ago, when you asked about someone, he or she was described in terms of character and personality. "Now," she lamented, "people say 'he's got a new car,' 'he owns a big house,' or 'he makes a lot of money.' "

In Papua New Guinea, Suzuki adds, "people and communities who have always grown or gathered their own food are being deceived, seduced or bribed to become part of the global economy. Cash crops such as coffee provide money, but then food must be bought from somewhere else. Here the waters teem with fish, yet the country is a major importer of canned mackerel from Taiwan." Most disturbing to Suzuki is global capitalism's disregard for the way Papuans have customarily understood their environment. Treating land as a commodity would be as ridiculous as buying and selling a family member or a bodily limb, he observes. "The global economy is changing that."

Thus the deception of the word "globalization." Its imagery of arms stretched across yawning oceans suggests a diffusion of power when, in fact, the opposite is occurring. Far from slowing down and spreading out, the norm-setting power of a few is accelerating with each new trade pact.

Not long before unveiling the final text of the 1988 Free Trade Agreement (FTA) between Canada and the U.S., Canada's trade minister, Pat Carney, said that her administration wanted to seal a deal "to ensure that in the future there is not the kind of anti-investment policies of other governments ... The changes which are brought in by this government are designed to stand the test of time." Tariffs schmariffs; the political appeal of the FTA was that it set the norm for later generations of Canadians.

Then came the North American Free Trade Agreement (NAFTA). Public administration professor Fred Bienefeld of Carleton University describes NAFTA as a regional project with no ambition to establish a parliament that would mediate between commerce and people. He warns that by entering such a trading bloc, countries that have managed to reconcile the free market and the public interest jeopardize their capacity to maintain that dignified compromise. In particular, these successful societies risk pandering to the insecurities and failures of the established powers.

A close friend of mine had a discussion with a senior trade negotiator in the U.S. The American told him, "Of course we understand that Japanese industrial policy has been very successful. But we don't think we can duplicate those policies in the United States, so we have to force the Japanese to abandon those policies." Here's a process where the less successful economies are using political power and even implicit military threats to coerce the more successful economies into abandoning the very things that made them successful.

Now there is talk of a transatlantic free trade agreement (TAFTA) among countries of the European Union and members of NAFTA. The implications if it is implemented? According to TAFTA booster and former U.S. trade representative Clayton Yeutter, "uncooperative developing countries would face a rapidly diminishing set of choices—basically either to sign up or go it alone without attractive access to U.S. and EU markets. Most would fall in line behind a more open agenda." Malaysian Prime Minister Mahathir bin Mohamad has made the same point, *sans* Yeutter's enthusiasm: "With their trading clout, the EU-NAFTA confederation could dictate terms to the rest of the world."

Like the breakthrough-achieving women who bend to the culture in an attempt to belong—but who can never bend enough to ensure belonging—so do developing countries wriggle within a trap. To be included in the latest round of global trade discussions, they have accepted market-driven measures under pressure from the same countries that today plan to devise new rules without them. Rather than being treated as partners, then, developing countries remain categorized as the Second or Third Worlds—always one notch below the First World masters. Sounds suspiciously like identity politics at work.

This dynamic between developing countries and global capitalism on the one hand, and between the breakthrough women and patriarchy on the other, mimics the dynamic between someone like me and religious orthodoxy: either I deny my queerness to gain entrance into the club of the Chosen or I accept my queerness, guarantee excommunication and forge my own, less sure, path. Similarly in certain feminist cabals: either you proclaim yourself a lesbian or you sign on for irrelevance at best, a psychological pelting at worst. In all cases, the either/or caveat is clear.

To use Clayton Yeutter's phrase, either the marginal "fall in line" behind an established norm or they forgo their few opportunities to participate. Identities are thus dictated, categories hardened, participation made less meaningful and the possibilities of belonging shrivelled.

An ethos of belonging demands that the either/or culture be transformed. But to what? As I have tried to demonstrate, everybody does identity politics. Affirms Michael Ignatieff, "We think of ourselves not as human beings first, but as sons, and daughters, fathers and mothers, tribesman, and neighbours. It is this dense web of relations and the meanings which they give to life that satisfies the needs which really matter to us." If that is true, then even without the motivation of superiority, people will hang on to their differences, because difference fulfills a deep-seated need to feel unique, special, at times precious.

There is something else to consider today. As the many facets of globalization pretend to blur the lines between us, the urge to distinguish ourselves becomes more compulsive. So we focus on our minor differences. What early twentieth-century psychiatrist Sigmund Freud called the "narcissism of small differences" has a contemporary bite—and it nips at Canada. Observes Ignatieff, "The differences between English and French Canada are tiny, when seen from the outside; but in the current mood of narcissistic self-justification on both sides, the risks of a spiral of rising intolerance are enormous."

An alternate vision of how to govern ourselves must account for each of these realities. Old-fashioned liberals such as Richard Gwyn and novelist Neil Bissoondath are selling illusions when they preach private celebrations of heritage and death to hyphenated nationality. Official multiculturalism or not, open immigration or not, the privatization of pluralism will not happen amid the trends I have described. Nor should it happen. A more honest ethos of belonging would encourage people to communicate small differences while bringing out our mutual dependence, binding us in a common culture of interaction.

Speaking of honesty, I have no idea how to realize that new ethos. This, though, I can say: The usual dichotomies are weighing us down. We have to switch direction.

. I I .

values

"The development of flexible identities is being spear-
headed by young Canadians. Like the values of the baby
boomers, their values will be exported to the wider society,
and perhaps, by the millennium, the boomers will get over
the shock that they are no longer the sole source of
novelty in the cultural universe."

—Pollster Michael Adams, <u>Sex in the Snow</u>, 1997

"By own hands freedom gained is freedom true / By
others freedom given is a captive doom."

—Poet Lesya Ukrainka, 1871–1913

INTRODUCTION

what can be reasonably
hoped for?

What can be reasonably hoped for?

Recognizing that our aspirations wrestle with our limitations, this question asks what can be done in the here and now. It is about strategies as much as solutions. And it is about stories. In this second part of my journey to belonging, I share the strategist's cap and the storyteller's chair with fifteen young Canadians. They become my co-travellers, unexpectedly guiding me through the impasse I reached in the previous pages.

A growing segment of our world calls itself, or could be called, marginal: it does not easily fit into the mainstream. To fashion a genuinely civil and democratic society, the marginal must interact with the mainstream. As important, they must perceive themselves to be interacting—that is, to be taken seriously.

But they are currently caught in a dilemma. On the one hand, the mainstream does not always accept their efforts. If the marginal want to belong, they have to bend so much that they cannot remain true to themselves. They are forbidden from bringing anything truly new to the table, so their participation is negated. On the other hand, if the marginal refuse to bend, and retrench into identity cliques as their only source of affinity, society will never be transformed. It will hurtle further towards calcified borders, a cynical public, unresponsive institutions and poisoned daily politics.

Hence the impasse. Given this panorama of power imbalances, and also given that cowboy capitalism, duplicitous socialism, religious absolutism, militant nationalism and ideological polarization all emanate from an either/or paradigm, can a plausible alternative be entertained?

For some insights, I turned to people who are making their way out of tough binds. My encounters uncovered more than mere survival tips for the marginalized. They led me to a stash of secrets about effective progressive politics. Chief among them: Personal values really do matter.

By "values," an admittedly loaded word, I only mean those principles that motivate people to certain behaviour. There is, of course, more to the enduring fascination with values than this bare-bones definition allows. In his famed search for democracy, eighteenth-century French philosopher Alexis de Tocqueville travelled to America and mined the newly formed nation for its animating mores. Finding the forces of family, religion and local participation, he called them "habits of the heart." But this phrase suggests that values are reflexive rather than deliberate. Indeed, a group of social scientists, trying to flesh out de Tocqueville's phrase by interviewing a wide swath of Americans twelve years ago, echoed his conclusion: "It turns out that values are the incomprehensible, rationally indefensible thing that the individual chooses when he or she has thrown off the last vestige of external influence." Born of unalloyed, self-indulgent freedom, values, by implication, are largely uncontrollable.

Not necessarily, cautions Richard Rorty, professor of humanities at the University of Virginia. Take selfishness, a value often paired with instinctive, law-of-the-jungle behaviour. Rorty says that selfishness can be "realistic" and "thoughtful" when compared, for example, to sadism—"the use of persons weaker than ourselves as outlets for our resentments and frustrations." Both selfishness and sadism cause needless suffering among others. But selfishness differs from sadism in being "less a matter of one's own self-worth and more a matter of rational calculation.

> If suburbanites cast their votes in favor of financing public education through locally administered property taxes, there will be less chance for the children in the cities to be properly educated, and so to compete with suburban children for membership in a shrinking middle class.

Such acts, Rorty shows, are not only selfish; they are premeditated. I, too, must disagree with the social scientists that values have no rational foundation. Instead of relying on their guts for guidance, my co-travellers are working out their values partly through emotional discipline towards others and partly through strategic self-interest. To quote one of them, "I'm very rational in my passions." In short, values can be thoughtfully celebrated by progressives no less than conservatives.

This discovery took me aback because, in my own hunt for justice, I have dismissed personal values as the fetish of fogies, a distraction from the *real* issues, or a guilt-built quest for virtue that involves unattainable goals and thus sets me up for perpetual inadequacy. Hardly dupes of doe-eyed moralists, however, my co-travellers embrace values as forces that induce them to think and not just feel. Many of them use the word "values" without flinching, making it as much their turf as that of the Christian Right. And, it turns out, values have long energized liberalism.

We would not know that by fixating on American conservatism's bouncing-baby "family values." Too many of us skim the recent record of the U.S. Republicans—their veto of a bill that would have raised the minimum wage to $4.55 over three years, their scuttling of a measure that would have funded abortions in incest and rape cases, their rejection of legislation that would have entitled parents to leave work for births and other medical urgencies, their subsequent Contract with America and its creeping influence on Canada—proclaim it all anti-family hypocrisy and wash our hands of the values thing.

These kinds of judgements not only gloss over the populist appeal of neo-conservatism, they also neglect the fact that family values have a glorious history in North America's progressive circles. As University of Chicago professor George Lakoff points out in *Moral Politics*, the nation-as-family metaphor that drives neo-conservatives has been the inspiration behind all sorts of social programs introduced by liberals. But where the neo-cons adopt a "Strict Father" model of the family, emphasizing reward and punishment from above (God and the state), liberals prefer a gender-neutral "Nurturant Parent" model, stressing discipline through respect between the vulnerable and the authoritative (children and parent, individuals and government).

The desire for stability and security characterizes both camps. Today, however, stability, security and the very notion of nation are under seige, posing challenges to both of these family models. How have the warring titans responded?

By and large, the old Left is so consumed with vanquishing a system which fosters economic insecurity that it clings to government as the only entity capable of chastening the multinationals. As a result, its most serious solutions arrive through the filter of a government fix-it, complete with a bureaucracy that erodes hands-on human participation.

In contrast, worthies of the new Right seldom criticize an economic system that disrupts the family's (and thus the nation's) stability by, for example, exporting jobs at thousands a clip. And when they have levelled such a criticism, as commentator Pat Buchanan did in his latest run for the Republican presidential nomination, the tone can best be described as insular and xenophobic.

Still, the new Right grasps human needs with an astuteness that the old Left lacks. By singling out inaccessible enemies—the Banks, the Corporate Agenda, Bay Street and Wall Street—the Left leaves individuals feeling immobilized to change anything. No wonder the language of victimhood seduces, then paralyses. It is here that the new Right has served public consciousness with its populist message of values.

Far from being "mean-spirited," which ascribes a strategically foolish motive, or "hostage to the rich and powerful," which implies a well-oiled conspiracy, many neo-conservatives want average people to enjoy power. After all, most neo-con sympathizers are ordinary folks. As such, they also accept what their neighbours sense: that in these topsy-turvy times, powers larger than ourselves determine economic and technological trends. In light of those limitations, what can we still control? Neo-cons offer personal values as the answer.

It follows that if we retain control over our own outlook, our own conduct, our own character, then each of us has an obligation—a personal responsibility—to exercise that control. Of course, translating personal responsibility into the society favoured by neo-conservatives demands that everybody abide by the Strict Father's rules. For reasons that will be clear later, this muscular morality is puffed-up cowardice; it evades the hardy challenges posed by belonging.

However, with respect to personal values being a ballast at a time of little direction, an oasis of order amid swirling change, I think the neo-cons are bang on. Other progressive minds might agree. In *The Politics of Meaning*, Michael Lerner blasts the old Left's "triumph of mechanistic thinking and de-spiritualization of daily life." Editor of the liberal Jewish magazine *Tikkun*, Lerner writes that "[b]ecause many progressive intellectuals and cultural critics fail to understand ... the powerful attraction of anything that seems to offer us the life energy that has been drained from so much of our economic and political and social life, these thinkers conclude that they are surrounded by people who are irrational at best." The working- and middle-class majority, "well aware of how contemptuously it is being treated, returns the favour."

And softens sympathy for fundamentalism. In his 1992 song "The Future," musician Leonard Cohen speculates about what happens when we try to control everything outside of ourselves but neglect to tame our inner impulses. The "order of the soul" overturns, he concludes, opening the door to fundamentalist sermonizing in a variety of venues, including his own stage. "Give me back the Berlin Wall / Give me Stalin and St. Paul," the lapsed liberal abruptly demands. "When they said REPENT / I wonder what they meant." Now Cohen knows. So, it seems, do countless voters.

To be sure, this need for some control can also be turned against fundamentalism. Lakoff sees "an emerging generation" of Republican women who are not afraid to challenge the anti-choice stalwarts. Given the global menaces to the family that they, on their own, cannot (or will not) oppose, these women view feminism as bringing some stability and security to the family by lending parents more control over upheavals such as unplanned pregnancies. If personal values cannot counter all powerlessness, they are more important than ever precisely because of the void they can fill.

Through our values, then, we may harness the need for some personal control to the service of collective belonging—again, provided those values make us think no less than feel. That is the key lesson I draw from my co-travellers. They are a varied lot, and plenty of values pepper my stories about them: humour, humility, self-respect, mutual respect, obligation, commitment, fairness and pragmatism, among others.

But like recurring threads, three values tie together their diverse lives: empathy, agency and accountability. Empathy gives people a stake in whittling away the walls of identity cliques. Agency helps them to realize that they can, not just should, participate beyond those cliques. And accountability reminds them of their own responsibilities as participants in the larger world.

Process always influences outcome, so allow me to explain how my contacts evolved. In a word, haphazardly. Throughout 1994–95, the cold calls I made, the newsletter ads I placed, the signatures I gathered at conferences and the private Rolodexes I raided landed me almost sixty names. I followed up, sometimes successfully, often not. (One woman—a fashion model with a disability—had just moved to Montana when I phoned. Her ex-boyfriend threatened to break my leg if I investigated her life story. In the end, it was not his threat, but the fact that I could not afford the trip to Montana, that weeded her out.) I also tried to explore francophone Quebec, native reserves and black Nova Scotia. Because of linguistic unfamiliarity or a wariness of journalists or clashing schedules, I emerged from these areas with few results.

Approximately half of all those I reached agreed to be interviewed over the phone. Judging by the insights their stories offered, I then asked some of them about visiting their homes and communities. Many said yes; various means of transportation eventually got me there, and I stayed in each place for at least two days.

The visits gave me a chance to get personal with my co-travellers, to survey their environments and just watch them "be." From the minutiae of body language to the mentally ill woman who woke me up at 4:30 a.m. and insisted that I evaluate her poetry, what I saw and heard at these pit stops reminded me that the people I am profiling are not angels who consistently practise their stated ideals. They are human beings with whom I sometimes disagree. But their empathy, agency and accountability give good value. Independent of each other, my co-travellers use these as tools to chisel out a significant space for themselves in society, even when society would rather they mind their own business on the margins. They have not obliged, and that is how they have grown to make freer choices, maximize their opportunities and live more democratically.

The next section looks at their personal epiphanies as much as their public activism. It begins by examining where progressive politics succeeds and where it deceives. The subsequent explorations of empathy, agency and accountability pave the way to a demonstration of how these values can work in tandem to produce concrete results and possibilities for broader, more enduring social change. Because each of these values is doable, each can be reasonably hoped for.

CHAPTER 4

to be progressive

Tzeporah Berman minced no words as she briefed the tense gathering of 400 people beneath a makeshift canopy on the edge of Clayoquot Sound, Vancouver Island. On this damp August night, the lanky Greenpeace campaigner asked how many of her fellow protestors would be willing to risk jail. About 150 hands went up, including that of sixteen-year-old Erin Davies. (The Ontario high school student later qualified her bravery: "I have to call my mother first." Mrs. Davies reluctantly gave her daughter the green light.)

To Erin and the others, Tzeporah issued a few tips. "We don't recommend that you resist arrest," she said. When being hauled to the police paddy wagon, "make sure you're never on your stomach. That can be very painful." Bring ID, pocket a few snack bars, avoid wearing necklaces but do wear several layers of clothing; the cell can be cold.

"This is a really important night for us," twenty-four-year-old Tzeporah reminded the motley group of grandmothers, doctors, overworked lawyers and underemployed renovators. "Tomorrow we're going to take the road, and the public forest will be back in the hands of the public." So began the biggest arrest ever in British Columbia: 209 people rounded up the next morning. So continued one of North American history's largest and most significant nonviolent demonstrations.

Significant not least because the Clayoquot summer of 1993 resurrected civil disobedience as a valid, indeed ethically compelling, response to corporate irresponsibility and government complacency. In April of that year, B.C. Premier Mike Harcourt decided to permit clear-cut logging in much of Clayoquot Sound, one of the few temperate rainforests left on earth. After his announcement, Tzeporah and nine others went to Clayoquot, dug toilets and unfurled protest banners. What motivated them is that, within its 325 hectares, Clayoquot epitomizes "biodiversity." In a voice so hushed that it undermines the stereotype of the leather-lunged lobbyist, Tzeporah explains biodiversity as "the hammock which sustains each of us." To clear-cut Clayoquot, she says, would be a symbolic assault on the ecosystem that allows us a decent quality of life, and an actual assault on the patch of land that teaches us how to maintain life itself. "So if we continue to clear-cut the forests, what we're doing is burning the library before we've even read the books."

For their part, loggers and industrialists wanted the book thrown at her. "[W]acked-out nature worshippers who pray to the moon," as the British Columbia Forest Alliance reportedly put it, were making business impossible. MacMillan Bloedel, a multinational logging company, tried at least twice to "get" Tzeporah in court. Each time, high-priced lawyers failed. Maybe more embarrassing for the B.C. foresters, journalists from around the world shoved cameras, tape recorders and microphones in her face every day. Tzeporah effectively told the logging industry where to stick its stumps.

In time, 12,000 people from all over the planet joined the camp she had helped to organize. Among the visitors were musicians Midnight Oil, attorney Robert Kennedy Jr. and California senator Tom Hayden, who wed the daughter of a B.C. logger. As news of the protest spread internationally, Premier Harcourt got an earful even from European trade partners. The accumulated pressure resulted in some redwood-tall triumphs. Harcourt's government banned conventional clear-cutting so that logging licences now meet tougher standards of approval. Moreover, an interim agreement awarded the Nuu-chah-nulth First Nations a say in the future of the sound—and thus of their ancestral territory.

Since then, Greenpeace has stepped up its campaign to give the old-growth forest a new lease on life. Although it has caught public flak and alienated a few of its own members, Tzeporah remains involved. Now based in San Francisco, she campaigns internationally for biodiversity.

The Clayoquot Sound protest was, for Tzeporah, a chance to enact core eco-feminist values. Eco-feminism, she says, "is the recognition that the domination of the environment is similar to the treatment of women in our society, and it's mutually reinforcing." The proof is in the politics we all share. The unquestioned concept of wilderness, Tzeporah suggests, comes from a time when Europeans resolved to tame the "evil forces of nature," as though nature had not been touched until their arrival. "Well, there are no areas of B.C. that have not been lived in by human beings," she states. "In a lot of remote areas, there's carbon-dated evidence of villages thousands of years ago. So, to a great extent, 'wilderness' is the product of a culture that says you can control nature, you can dominate other races, you can own women." (Tzeporah has noticed that related assumptions sprinkle the sado-sexual language of environmental activists: "a virgin forest," "rape of the land," "penetrating the pristine watershed.") Eco-feminism is meant to "get beyond this cultural heritage of 'strong' and 'weak.' "

Consequently, Tzeporah agrees that saving the earth cannot be as easy as substituting a matriarchy for the patriarchy. "People always try to force me into that: Do you think if women were in power, everything would be better? No, I don't. Clayoquot was about understanding that power is something to be shared by all, for all." Admittedly, this point sounds trite and tired. Consensus decision-making, the Achilles' heel of the Left, usually produces endless discussions about process and triggers an avalanche of inaction. But not at Clayoquot. Organizers applied this hoary trope to a contemporary case of realpolitik, coming up with a Peaceful Direct Action Code that "respected everyone's individuality while creating a sense of community." The code pledged, among other things, to avoid verbal and physical abuse, not to damage property, to reject weapons, to turn away alcohol or drugs from the camp and to strive for an atmosphere of calm and dignity. All who entered the camp were asked to abide by that declaration of nonviolence.

Ideological dilettantism be damned; the code made the camp accessible to a cross-section of people, ensuring enough numbers for a show of strength. Maintaining the basic values of respect and understanding "wasn't nearly as dramatic as blowing up a bridge," Tzeporah acknowledges. "There were some people who came to the camp wanting to do that—blow things up. But if the first images of the protest had been violent, I don't think parents would have wanted to bring their kids." Nor, for that matter, themselves. Had the Clayoquot campaign featured frenzied tree-spikers, lives would have been imperilled, public sympathy repelled and a government crackdown legitimized. Instead, the peace camp resonated the world over because it attracted diversity by accommodating it.

Being a microcosm of society, however, the camp did not escape the problems of society. A young person stepped forward in a "women's circle" to say that she had been sexually harassed by a male protestor. If true, this behaviour violated the code and demanded action. At the same time, Tzeporah explains, energy cannot be squandered when "you're getting up every morning at 3:30 and blockading a logging road and people are being arrested and you're trying to provide legal support and you're teaching people about rainforests and taking them there—and, on top of that, dealing with everyday emotional issues." But if camp organizers wanted visitors to leave with dreams of social change, they had to try addressing the nightmares. Their compromise: share the responsibility. Members of the women's circle approached some men with whom they knew they could candidly speak. "We asked them if they'd form their own circle and invite the harassers in. We named names. And we said, 'Look, as women we have to deal with this. We believe it's time that you, as men, also dealt with it.' "

The men agreed. They formed a circle and eventually asked two individuals to leave the camp. For Tzeporah and other women, supporting that decision "was a total role reversal because, in the past, the men had been very supportive of us. But supportive of *us*—you know, not taking anything on themselves. We finally said, 'Thanks for your support. Now you handle it.' "

Portraying it more as an opportunity than a crisis, Tzeporah calls the sexual harassment complaint a "turning point" in the camp. "[It] freed men to speak out as individuals. There's a groupthink that goes on in any community, so a lot of men wouldn't bring the harassment issue up. After this, feminism became their conversation and not just ours."

Evidently, a little power-sharing went a long way. Tzeporah recalls Amy, a fifteen-year-old girl who was "too shy to speak much when she got to the camp." Three months later, amid routine threats against the protestors, Amy walked through the camp with a hand-held radio, leading emergency workshops and overseeing some security. Says Tzeporah, "I don't think that would have happened unless men in the camp were willing to give her the space to take on a traditionally male role." Chalk one up for possibility.

Letters tell Tzeporah that Clayoquot restored a sense of possibility to many other lives. "I've gotten mail from people across the country who write, 'I'm back in my community and I've started an environmental group on this or a feminist group on that and thank you so much for the experience.' People were changed just by their ability to say, 'I have a choice.' " At this, her soft voice finally rises and exudes wonder. "It's amazing, but I think our culture is so passive that to be able to say, 'I have the freedom to stand on that road, I have the freedom to go to jail'—it irreversibly affected I don't know how many protestors."

Defying passivity is an evolving strategy for Tzeporah. When she debates corporate PR teams and burly union leaders, she could stick to the cold facts—that, for instance, every grapple-yarder (clear-cutting machine) costs five human jobs, rendering logging companies B.C.'s biggest *dis*employers over the last decade. Or she could direct hard questions at the public conscience: Where was justice when former premier Harcourt informed Europeans that his government was "ending colonialism" while 60 per cent of Clayoquot's people live on 0.4 per cent of the land base, endure a 70 per cent unemployment rate and suffer runaway suicide?

But Tzeporah believes that her effectiveness as an activist stems less from her command of data than from having lived environmental tragedy.

"My mother died when I was fifteen and my father when I was fourteen, both from what I would characterize as environmentally related illnesses," she says. "My father had heart problems and my mother had cancer." The Berman children spent the next five years functioning as a tiny community. "My two sisters and I refused adoption for my brother, fought off all these people and eventually had enough money left over from my parents to keep the house. After that, we worked by consensus. We shared the household tasks and made all the decisions together."

When decision-making broke down, the family drew from the reserve strength of their relationships. Particularly "healing" for Tzeporah was the communication with her older sister. "Probably because I was sixteen, I was in a totally rebellious stage. Maybe I shouldn't have been drinking until four in the morning, but even though we disagreed wildly on so many things, we talked honestly. I could always say, 'I feel like crying, I really miss Mom.' If we hadn't had that commitment to talk and listen, I don't think our little community would have lasted. So community, responsibility and democracy are very personal notions for me. They're not at all abstract."

Because these values have proven their worth to her, Tzeporah is determined to embody them beyond the private realm—even if that means jettisoning her comfortable caricatures of opponents. "Something which recently hit me is how I objectify others without even knowing it," she admits. "I was on a debate panel with a logger's wife, and just dreading it because I had no clue what she was going to say. When we actually sat down, I was shocked to have this woman before me, this really nice-looking person in a pale pink sweater. It didn't square with the image in my head—you know, She-Logger from Hell." Tzeporah arrived at a stunning revelation—the logger's wife "is a real person with real experiences that have brought her to this place. I have to respect that. We've got differences of opinion to overcome but that's only possible once we quit demonizing each other."

To be progressive, Tzeporah has learned, is literally to move ahead; not merely to theorize forward, nor simply to protest against, but to face one's covert conservatism and snap out of the intellectual lethargy it induces. Truly progressive politics, then, knows when to leave the insulating clutch of doctrine. It is a contemporary imperative, because as the most unlikely candidates become our neighbours, "common sense" certainties are the veils that prevent vision.

Two young Muslim sisters with lightly freckled faces, funky bracelets and brightly dyed head scarves passionately unite Islam and feminism over breakfast at Montreal's landmark Jewish deli, Ben's. At the time, Afra and Mariam Jalabi are progressive activists and political science students at McGill University. I have contacted them because I want to know why committed advocates of gender equality would wear *hijab*, the headdress decreed by Islamic canon law to signal female modesty. In the course of our conversation, I discover that the many layers of their lives do not lend Afra and Mariam to easy generalization. They choose to cover their heads, have willingly married and defend both institutions. Afra, twenty-seven, takes no offence at women who publicly bare their breasts if that is how they want to "desexualize" their bodies. She, however, approaches the problem differently. Mariam, twenty-five, has married a white Canadian. She hopes to start a fashion institute in the Middle East as an expression of post-colonial chic, producing designs that will permeate the boundaries between Western and Eastern tastes, as well as between history and the future.

Consequently, it annoys Afra and Mariam that when Quebec feminists look at them, all they seem to see is hijab. "What I wear is a matter of practicality," Afra says. "I don't want to be defined by hijab all my life. My identity is much more fluid than that." (Hence her hesitation to be profiled in this book and her request to have that hesitation noted. "A book is a finished product but identity is a process. Even after this book is done, I'll be changing and moving on.") Tradition seems more the obsession of others than of the Jalabi sisters.

Especially in the ping-pong ethnic politics of contemporary Quebec. Witness, for example, the Montreal-area public schools that, in 1994, kicked out two Muslim students for observing hijab, expulsions backed to no small degree by nationalist organizations, newspaper editorialists and teachers' unions. (One of the schools implemented a strict dress code *after* the Muslim student enrolled. Both schools are run by Catholic boards. Subsequently, the Montreal Catholic School Commission ignored the Quebec Human Rights Commission, which ruled any hijab ban to be illegal.) Witness, as well, the Muslim School of Montreal, which required all female teachers, including non-Muslims, to don hijab in the name of reinforcing Islamic values. (The school principal insisted that each of the female teachers knew this to be a condition of employment. None, he said, voiced opposition. No matter, retorted Fatima Houda-Pepin, a Liberal member of Quebec's National Assembly. She argued that the condition itself constituted an "assault" on Canada's Charter of Rights and Freedoms. Houda-Pepin spoke not just as a politician but also as a practicing Muslim.) Above all, recall the words of former Quebec premier Jacques Parizeau. On referendum night in October 1995, when he directed blame at the "ethnic vote" for helping to defeat his separatist forces, Parizeau was targeting people like the Jalabis—who, it turns out, are not ready federalists.

Over the past two years, in fact, Afra's sympathies have heightened for Quebec's attempt to preserve its language. The reason? Living in Ottawa, where she is now completing a Master's degree in journalism, has opened her eyes to the Anglo tilt of Canada's capital city. Still, both Jalabis handle the corrosive beast of nationalism with asbestos gloves. Born in Syria, raised partly in Germany and recently emigrated from Saudi Arabia, they shuttle between Canada and the Middle East—a practice that their mother has long encouraged to avoid romanticizing cultures.

How vexing, then, that to many Québécois, Afra and Mariam would be symbols of a hated multiculturalism. Hated not only because this policy emanates from enemy territory, Ottawa, and was legislated by a supposed turn-coat, Pierre Trudeau, but because it clashes with the provincial policy of interculturalism. "You have a patchwork or mosaic in multiculturalism," opined Madelaine Lussier, a senior Quebec official, in 1994. "But with interculturalism, you have a common state." Quixotically presented to newcomers as a "moral contract," the paramountcy of the French language and the sovereignty of the National Assembly are not up for negotiation. Interculturalism, by Lussier's own analogy, parrots the melting pot ardour of the United States.

Not surprisingly, the Jalabis claim to confront in Montreal much more racism than sexism, yet racism less from male bus drivers and elderly shopkeepers than from feminists who do not (or will not) understand the rights that Islam gives women. For example, by Mariam's interpretation, Islam recognizes women to be as sexual as men. Therefore, it views physical fulfillment as a realistic, healthy and natural priority in marriage; children and other family obligations come later. As corresponding rights, Muslim women may refuse marriage or impose conditions on their agreement to marry. Mariam did. She may visit her family anytime, with her husband, David, footing the travel bill. Mariam and David also have equal access to divorce papers. While Muslim women are entitled to a just financial settlement upon divorce, inheritance rights, too, are balanced with men's. Although daughters inherit less than sons, women are not obliged to spend their inheritance on anybody, Mariam informs. Nor is anybody permitted to touch women's assets. By contrast, men must provide for their families, including parents.

To be sure, the male responsibility to provide presumes patriarchal authority. But Afra points out that "when western feminists object, what they're often telling me is, 'Our patriarchy is superior to your patriarchy.' In both worlds, patriarchy still exists. Unfortunately, they don't see the connection between Muslim women's struggles and their own."

Quebec feminists usually assume that the Jalabi sisters take an interest in feminism because, as Afra recounts hearing, " 'you must have had really horrible experiences as women in the Middle East.' " She tells them otherwise. "My father, my uncles, my cousins saw women as equals. My parents even discussed ideas with me as a child. Growing up, I felt that Gandhi, Tolstoy and Socrates were my personal friends." Afra realized only after moving away from home that women rarely enjoyed the respect to which the Jalabi girls were accustomed. Without wearing the label on her sleeve, she became a feminist upon entering the real Western world. "I saw the horrors and said, 'Oh my goodness, we have to change this.'"

Canadians, she found out, had a ways to travel before treating every-one as individuals. When Afra arrived in Montreal to attend university, she rented a room from a woman who called herself a strong feminist and objected to hijab. Schooled in the liberal arts, this woman had studied French literature, earned a graduate degree in industrial relations and even worked at a human rights commission. According to Afra, "Her big argument was: If your men wore scarves, I would accept your way of dressing. So I told her: If your men wore lipstick and heels …"

On another occasion the woman told light-skinned Afra that she could look "very Canadian" if only she would lose her hijab. "So I asked, 'What's that supposed to mean?' She was saying that to look Canadian, you have to look white; to *be* Canadian, you have to be white. That hurt," Afra volun-teers. She wonders how the woman expected her to respond. "'Oh, thank you, I've been looking for ways to have white skin'? I know that inside I'm not a 'white' woman. I might as well deal with that reality on the outside."

Still, Afra credits her roommate for candour. "At least she said what she was thinking, which gave me a chance to say something back. I'm tired of certain comments but sometimes it's the silence that kills, the contemplating silence that kills." Because few Canadians articulate their racism—politeness and all that—when Afra started the search for another apartment, she knew to ask upfront if her hijab offended. "Here, in a supposedly liberal society," she notes with a spritz of irony, "I was in the position of having to gain approval for my style of clothing."

Since coming to Canada, Afra believes she has put her finger on a key problem with so-called progressive politics: "The *ideals* of Western soci-eties are always contrasted and compared to the *actuality* of other soci-eties—rather than ideals compared to ideals, actuality compared to actuality. If you want to say that Muslim women are oppressed, then tell me what's happening here to Western women. Tell me about the level of abuse in the legal system, the housing situation for single mothers, the chances of pay equity for career women, the preoccupation with looking 'presentable.' Compare clitoridectomy to plastic surgery. Why do we say one is a 'mutilation' and the other is an 'operation'?"

Every culture is kinetic, she says. So when critics intone that hijab ought to be mothballed, they are treating Islamic cultures like a musty trunk of rituals, ignoring the internal debates and inherent dynamism. In that vein, Afra observes that although the U.S. constitution reflects an eighteenth-century ideal of society, nobody calls on Americans to dump the document because it is "traditional" or "out of date." Rather, progressive activists in every generation seek constitutional amendments. "But Muslims are told that the only way to deal with traditions like hijab is to throw them out. Not modify them, the way I have by being creative with my scarves. When we match reality with reality, maybe we can start evaluating things a little bit more accurately."

Perhaps too polite a Canadian to call it hypocrisy, Afra says that this "inconsistency of analysis" imposes a burden on Muslim women that often shuts them down. "Not all of us are able to answer back" to the myths and mental somersaults, she attests. "I don't think every Muslim woman should have to be a scholar to live here with dignity. She should be able to just be respected."

Maybe so, I answer, but authentic respect cannot be forced. It does not have to be, Afra replies. As an example, she cites her reaction to Gwen Jacob, a University of Guelph student who went topless in 1991, got arrested for indecent exposure, inspired nationwide demonstrations by bra-challenged women, and defied legal priggishness to the point of breastfeeding in court while appealing her conviction. I remember women receiving Jacob with smirks and giggles, the prudery of many a feminist exposed. Afra, however, surprised her friends. "I told them, 'I see Gwen Jacob's point,' because I agree with fighting the senseless sexualization of our bodies as long as it's not just for shock value." Muslim women may choose to contribute to this fight by putting on clothes instead of peeling them off, but the common issue is how women's bodies are manipulated by moral purists and turned into battlefields, not just between men but also between women. "If I can tolerate Jacob's stand," Afra asks, "why can't Western feminists tolerate my position?"

Feminism, Afra suggests, can be more of an orthodoxy than the religions it ridicules. "[T]he way I perceive myself as a Muslim is far less institutionalized than the way my former roommate practised her feminism. No humility. No humanity." As such, Afra would sooner elevate "a just patriarch than a small-minded feminist woman." I humbly submit to her that any world view which disallows individual ignorance teeters on a theological arrogance of its own. Ignorance, she clarifies, cannot be disallowed; it is too human to avoid. But ignorance itself demystifies nothing. It can and should be channelled into some measure of open-mindedness. "I'm not talking about total relativism," Afra assures. "We have to make judgements in order to live sane lives. We can make informed judgements, though; compassionate judgements."

Compassion, although often construed as unconditional love for others, is actually Afra's strategy for self-preservation. "I try not to be put into a corner where all of my psychological or emotional reactions are set up by people who misunderstand me. I would rather go out of my way to show compassion; to say, 'I care and I want to improve things for both of us.' But I'm not going to get angry at you [because] I won't let you be the only one deciding things here." In spite of her proclamations to the contrary, Afra's furrowed brow and sharp tone reveal some anger. "I do have some anger inside me," she later admits, "but as [African-American feminist writer] Audre Lorde used to say, anger can be a motivating force as long as it doesn't become hatred. So even when I fight, I fight with quiet confidence. Compassion is a sign of confidence that says: This is me."

The peaceful expression of uniqueness also fuels Mariam's dream to establish a Middle East fashion institute—something Audre Lorde surely did not expect. This dream seems an unusual response to racism because it charts a road less well travelled than that of reciprocal prejudice. It recasts dress as only one dimension of women's identity, highlights hijab as a tradition not immune to change and broadens the tradition to embrace the many cultures of a fractured region. In turn, the fashion institute could serve as an outlet for other women's creativity. "Today, there are so many styles of hijab in Egypt and Syria, it tells me that women really want to be themselves," Mariam says.

"Women want to choose again," affirms Afra. "Clothing in the Middle East evolved in relation to the heat and the sun and the sand. It was a process that colonization mutilated. It took choices away."

"Since all the new styles are still coming from the West," Mariam adds, "this crazy idea came to my mind: I'm in the West already, I'm sewing for me and Afra because we can't find the kind of modest covering that we need here—why not apply to a design institute after I graduate from my political studies in Montreal? I would love New York, I think. [Then] I can go back to the Middle East and redesign clothing." This year, Mariam began attending classes at Manhattan's Fashion Institute of Technology. Her aim is to integrate cutting-edge style with the practicality that women once had and still need. "It could be so beautiful," Mariam fantasizes, "so exciting."

And the time could be right because, as she grasps it, "the peace process is changing the whole mentality of the Middle East. In Israel, devout Jewish women wear scarves on their head, and I'm thinking: When the borders open, how will that influence the way Arab and Jewish women see themselves?" Notwithstanding last year's election of Prime Minister Benjamin Netanyahu, whose speeches declare a preference for Israeli security rather than regional peace, Mariam hopes that "the borders won't matter much in a hundred years." But she stays vigilant. Whether in fashionable politics or in the politics of fashion, "I don't want to replace one colonialism with another. We have to move beyond that."

For Tzeporah Berman, feminism is a valid vehicle of social change. For the Jalabi sisters, too much about feminism is static and thereby repressive. Their perspectives need not contradict each other. Tzeporah traces the domination of our environment to a European heritage that separates the earth and its creatures into superior and inferior classes; it is a heritage which she says we have to "get beyond." Similarly, Afra and Mariam observe Western feminism's inclination to control, manipulate, even mutilate, out of ideological conceit. They urge feminists to "move beyond that." Tzeporah warns against replacing the patriarchy with a matriarchy. Likewise, decrying the white man's burden in the name of white women's presumed superiority is no signpost of progress to the Jalabis. And just as Tzeporah has learned that "the other" can be a complex individual, so Afra and Mariam want every feminist to realize the absurdity of shrinking them to shrouds.

In short, we have not really gotten over the imperialist impulse of yesterday's politics. But we must, because a planet of simultaneously porous yet congealing borders is making identity more nuanced and belonging more tricky.

Afra pinpointed the value that can begin to form a new politic: compassion. I call it empathy. It is what Afra had when she recognized Gwen Jacob's point and it is how Tzeporah came to view her debate opponent as a human being. Empathy transforms the foreign into the familiar by turning the mirror on ourselves. The changes it can spark ought not to be underestimated.

CHAPTER 5

empathy

For Thomas Ponniah, it was the scenic route to political transformation. He once followed his buddies to strip joints in Montreal; he now teaches human rights to students of community work at George Brown College in Toronto. If a former jock can have a "feminist awakening," the twenty-nine-year-old points out, there is hope for empathy among many more of us.

His youth would not have attested to that optimism. As a child, Thomas daily watched his mother insult his father's manhood and saw his father call his mother a bitch. "But," he emphasizes, "when it came to me, both parents were very loving, and that emotional stability gave me the independence to think for myself." As an adolescent, Thomas cultivated a set of Christian ethics that put spirituality ahead of sexuality.

Until his talent for soccer got noticed. Between the ages of twelve and seventeen, Thomas was chosen to tend goal for the Montreal inner-city squad La Chine Cosmos. In wintertime, he replaced his soccer cleats with hockey skates. Born in India and brown in skin colour, Thomas took up sports as a way of fitting in. He had to do something, Montreal not being a city known for racial peace and teens not being a group known for open-mindedness. "People called me a nigger," Thomas says. "Paki wasn't in vogue yet."

He also joined his teammates at strip joints after practice. Despite his ambivalence about being in the cheesy barroom darkness amid the thrusting and hooting of his pals, Thomas grew familiar with an irony of belonging: acting sexist helped dissolve the racial boundaries between him and the other boys. "When you're feeling alienated as a man of colour, sexism and homophobia give you tools of bonding with the so-called mainstream. They're your tickets to temporary inclusion," he explains. "If you're constantly being told that you're not masculine, that you're not human, that you're not enlightened, then sexuality is one of the few areas that you feel you have to control." He continued patronizing strip clubs as a university undergrad, remembering himself "still not strong enough to say no."

After bending so much to belong, Thomas might well have wound up living a series of phony roles to bond his way out of racism. But the likelihood of that changed the year he learned about concrete threats of anti-black violence. In November 1987, Montreal endured a major episode of racial friction triggered by a police shooting. Anthony Griffin, a black man and sometime burglary suspect, had been arrested for refusing to pay a cab fare. When he tried to bolt from the cruiser in the parking lot of the police station, Constable Allan Gosset shot Griffin in the head, killing the unarmed nineteen-year-old. Although Gosset swore that his gun had gone off accidentally, it was not his first attack on someone black: in 1981, the Quebec Human Rights Commission sued Gosset for severely beating a Ghanaian business professor, who lost his eyesight for two weeks thereafter. That case ended in an out-of-court settlement of $2,450. Not so in the Griffin incident. Charged with manslaughter, Gosset underwent two criminal trials—and was acquitted, both times, by an all-white jury. In between acquittals, the police union frustrated Chief Roland Bourget's bid to fire Gosset, allowing the controversial constable to take early retirement.

"L'affaire Gosset," as it came to be known, shook Thomas to his core. "I started to think seriously about racism," he says in a moment of massive understatement. "There was no reason to shoot [Griffin]. The guy put his hands up and the cop fired anyway." Over the next year, Thomas heard other stories about young men of colour being hassled or assaulted, with little or no police accountability. Soon enough, he had his own encounter to tack onto the list.

Thomas was heading home after attending a play at Montreal's National Theatre School. He had to cross several blocks of ill-lit residential streets to reach his basement room in Westmount. At 11:00 p.m., only a few blocks from his door, a police cruiser pulled up and stopped him. In a city-wide atmosphere of anxiety, the unprovoked approach of police alarmed Thomas. "I told myself, 'No matter what, don't get into that car.' "

Wearing a short coat, Thomas stood outside for half an hour in −25° F weather. Meanwhile, the police grilled him, pretending to check his records on their computer. "First question: 'Have you ever been stopped by the police?' " he remembers them inquiring. "I said, 'No.' Ten minutes later: 'Have you ever been stopped by the police?' 'No.' Ten minutes later: 'Have you ever been stopped by the police?' It's this intimidation game, right? They want you to get frustrated and say, 'Fuck off' or something like that so they can claim that 'he resisted.' " Finally, one of the officers asked Thomas what he studied at university. Political science, he replied. At this, they sat up—political science students had been prominent in organizing protests against the brutality of Montreal police. "They looked at each other for a second," Thomas recounts. "Two minutes later they said, 'The computer shows nothing' and they let me go." He adds that he heard no sounds from their computer.

What left the most indelible impression on Thomas were the nuances of that situation: he felt both lifted and disempowered at the same time. "It's amazing how you can be a well-educated individual, yet suddenly realize how vulnerable you are to the world," he says. "But because those cops believed I could do something to show them up, I gained a certain power." Thus began his political transformation. In the literal sense, Thomas absorbed more of the world. Trekking through Europe in the summer of 1989, as France revelled in the two hundredth anniversary of its republican revolution and the iron curtain of the Eastern bloc folded into a million fragments, Thomas imbibed the euphoria—and possibility—of political change.

Then came his feminist awakening. In December 1989, Canada reeled from the so-called "Montreal Massacre," a gunman's murder of fourteen female engineering students whom he presumed to be feminists and blamed for usurping his spot on the class roster. Thomas sensed solidarity with the shooting victims. They had been singled out not for their actions but for their appearance, not for what they had done but for what they were perceived to have done. In stringing together his own experiences with violence, from the scarring verbal sexism of his parents to the lethal racism of police, Thomas became, in his phrase, "pro-feminist."

The transformation entailed posing a grim and honest challenge to himself. "If I'd walked into my classroom and been ordered, as a man, to leave so these women could be directly in the line of fire, what would I have done?" he wonders. "I can't say for certain that I would have disarmed

the [gunman]."There is reason for entertaining such challenges. Empathy, he suggests, emerges bit by bit out of "self-questioning."

Since asking himself a plethora of questions, Thomas has reached some temporary conclusions. "One truth about human beings is that we have a basic desire to express ourselves as well as to be heard," he believes. "So to build a society that's more human, less hierarchical, we've got to have communities communicating rather than dominating."

I observed him demonstrate that lesson in class. When students made comments, he took pains to write their words—not his—on the board. "Students should see their exact thoughts going up," Thomas insists. "I never put down a student. I never say, 'That's wrong.' I always say, 'Try to clarify that.' Or when two students have a disagreement, I say, 'Let's understand the values behind each side.' What I'm saying there is, 'Both of you have good points; now let's see how they fit into the broader scheme of things.' "

More important, perhaps, he starts each semester with "ice-breakers," from name games to physical exercises, to build classroom empathy. "That way, the students immediately see each other as human beings, so when I do get around to talking about gender or race or sexuality, they recognize these categories as only part of their identity, not their whole identity. And when a person makes a sexist remark, the others in the class can say, 'Well, that was an ignorant moment, but on the whole this is a person worth listening to.' "

Besides offering us second chances, empathy can be central to expressing our full selves, Thomas notes. "I once argued with a woman I was going out with about the fact that her feminism seemed kind of flimsy. She said, 'The thing with you is, when you say something anti-racist, your friends support you. If I say something feminist, my friends call me a bitch.' " That exchange proved something of a revelation for Thomas, whose friends are his "human community." In particular, "I have two very close male friends who know where I'm coming from when I talk to them about my relationships. They can ask me, 'Are you being sexist here?' or 'Are you trying to dominate her?' and I don't feel defensive." Thomas says this capacity for closeness springs from a shared willingness to abandon some male precepts and just be themselves for the moment.

Another friendship, with a "radical lesbian," has inspired Thomas to be an unofficial pioneer of sexless intimacy. "One time, Anurima was over and we were talking in my room. I had two mattresses put together on the floor. I was lying on one, she was stretched out on the other, and we both just fell asleep. After that, we started to hold each other, like a couple. Even though she's attractive, it never crossed my mind to come on to her. Maybe that's because she's an open dyke, but I think there's more to it. Rima told me about being sexually assaulted as a girl and that conversation stayed in my head. When I held her, I felt I was holding my sister."

As a pro-feminist man, Thomas tries to relate to women in their totality as human beings—"not just their form," he stresses, "but their content, too." This level of empathy is no mean feat because, says Thomas, sexuality saturates North American culture. "If a guy is straight and preoccupied with sexuality, then he probably won't interact with a woman he's drawn to without seeing her as this conquest-in-waiting. At some point, part of him thinks, 'I wonder if I can get her to sleep with me.'" So it saddens, but hardly shocks, him that a man and a woman who are friends will not have their arms around each other in the presence of their lovers. "As long as our attitude gives primacy to sexuality," Thomas reckons, "we're going to be sexist."

Hence the reactions of supposedly progressive men and women to his affectionate, yet platonic, relationship with Rima. "Men say, 'Aren't you frustrated? You must get aroused.' And women—feminists—say, 'It makes no sense.' One woman said to me, 'I'd never sleep with a man in that position'—hugging, she means." All of those comments drove home to Thomas that "in this society, our presumed identity is [as] sexual beings, not [as] human beings." In films from India, he adds, when a brother and sister show each other fondness, westerners often take it as sublimated incest. "Why," Thomas wonders, "should our range of experiences be so limited?"

His range of experiences includes a relationship in which both partners could sleep with other women and men, leading him to a startling nugget of self-knowledge. "The anxiety it caused to picture my girlfriend with another man—my sexual possessiveness—really surprised me," Thomas laughs. "Even though I wasn't overtly jealous, it hit me that a central part of heterosexual monogamy is the expectation that men can sleep around and women can't." By becoming conscious of this, Thomas says, he began to free himself from the need to dominate. I ask for an example or twelve. "The woman I'm currently seeing is someone who explores herself on a number of levels, and I love that." At least he thinks he does. "I do occasionally get a little jealous. I'm sure there's a voice within that doesn't want a woman to be more 'successful,' whatever that means, but acknowledging that is part of being transformed."

Thomas also acknowledges self-interest behind the effort to infuse his masculinity with empathy. "I'm reinventing my manhood because I want the power to explore all kinds of experiences and experience all kinds of emotions. A truly free person isn't someone who says, 'Monogamy? Of course I'm monogamous'; it's someone who wants to know the alternatives, the human possibilities."

Which is why he calls for empathy in politics—to realize the possibilities for freedom en masse. Thomas says the times are ripe for a sweeping democratic movement. We live in a period of enormous suspicion of the state, resentment towards politicians, defiance of traditional authorities. But, hibernated in our biologically correct cliques, we neglect to help build a popular base for democracy.

"If someone walks into a room and announces, 'The single biggest problem is white people' or 'The single biggest problem is the corporate agenda' or 'The single biggest problem is patriarchy,' how can there be a genuine discussion?" Thomas asks. "When a white male does something progressive, it's because he has 'white male privilege.' When he does something regressive, it's also because he's a 'privileged white male.' He can't win." The upshot is that some of us give this guy no room to change; we just implicate him. Then, when we say we will not spend time educating him, we continue to implicate him. All of which assumes that we have nothing to learn from him.

Thomas considers that assumption misguided. "If you see things in monolithic ways, there will be no metamorphosis. As soon as you say, 'I'm a person of colour, therefore I'm *completely* victimized and white people are the source of all my problems,' you can't have a vision. You're so busy reacting against what you conceive of as white power that, in a sense, you're giving someone else power over you." To develop a vision of transformation and not just resistance, Thomas says, we have to begin with the belief that all of us share something: a common desire to choose our destinies. "And my choices as a man *will* involve, *have* to involve, your choices as a woman, or as a black person, or as a gay, or whatever. The only way we can be free is to be free together. So everyone has experiences and ideas we can learn from."

Hold on, I interject. How do you know that we all share something?

Thomas cites Buddhist monk and Nobel Peace Prize nominee Thich Nhat Hanh as saying that below this world of difference and separation is a common ocean of being. Our outer identities are only ripples on the ocean.

Fine, I shrug, but how do you know that his interpretation is not so much New Age Pablum? "During the Crusades," Thomas answers, "the Muslims and Christians hated each other, right? They were all out killing each other. At the same time, though, Muslim scholars and Christian clerics corresponded with each other. Beneath that veneer of violence was a mutual search for truth." Ministers Falwell and Farrakhan: Are you listening?

As political activists, Thomas says, we cannot forget the violent side of this story, but as human beings we have to emphasize the visionary side of it. He strikes the balance by remembering that "social transformation won't come strictly from marching and picketing. You also have to create a trust in intuition, spirituality and experience—other people's experiences as well as your own." That is the reason Thomas treasures friends such as Rima. "Since there's no sexual thing happening, we hang together out of genuine interest in each other."

He believes this approach can pull many social justice coalitions back from the brink of emotional meltdown and intellectual myopia. "We've got to be genuinely interested in each other's fates so we're not stomping out of the room at the first blow to our specific cause. Human beings can be negotiated with; categories can't."

The empathy that Thomas Ponniah describes is more than a capacity to look beyond ourselves; it is a *willingness* to do so. Whether he senses solidarity with the victims of the Montreal Massacre or teaches his students to recognize each other as worthy of being listened to, Thomas is advocating empathy. When he fosters a closeness with his male friends and comforts a vulnerable woman with brotherly overtures rather than macho come-ons, Thomas is practising empathy. Above all, when he thinks seriously about racism after the fatal shooting of a young black man, Thomas is actually wondering: Will I be next? His empathy is born of self-preservation but his subsequent actions as an anti-racist help protect the lives of countless people beyond himself.

Empathy, then, is not altruistic love. Nor can empathy be equated to generosity, which suggests a degree of selflessness that is more than what should be expected. Rather, empathy serves the self as much as anyone else. It is a willingness to relate to the situation of others as if it were our own; to make the links between ourselves and that which we see around us. By making those links, we draw ourselves into the situations of others, so that we now have a stake—a self-interest, really—in ensuring that they are cared about. Recognizing my self-interest does not guarantee that I will act, but it does make the possibility of acting (and acting effectively) more probable. As such, self-interest is harnessed for a larger good, preventing it from oxidizing into selfishness.

This is where neo-conservatives lose me. They rightly claim that we have control over ourselves, but their claim too readily gets bastardized into the belief that we have no responsibility for anything outside of ourselves. Even *Globe and Mail* editor William Thorsell, often labelled a neo-con, exposes this cult of individualism in criticizing the "American dream" theme touted by U.S. Republicans (and, I will add, mimicked by their Canadian admirers):

> [A focus on the American dream] is repressive because it insists that any individual's failure to succeed (measured by career and money) is a private matter, with no social roots. The American dream makes an *a priori* assertion that the fundamental assumptions and conditions of U.S. society are fine. So when you buy into the dream, you give up the basis of any serious criticism of the society that serves as the vehicle for the dream. Serious critiques are personal. Personal "renewal" is the route to success.

This dependence on personal renewal is why, despite spinning a good line about responsibility and community, neo-conservatives rarely take responsibility for the social implications of their policies. When they say homelessless has nothing to do with their policies, they mean homelessness has nothing to do with the *failure* of their policies. If the aim of neo-conservative measures is personal renewal, then the sole determinant must be personal will. Their cult of individualism ignores the paradox that we cannot be individuals on our own; our actions always have consequences for others and, therefore, barriers to personal success exist outside of ourselves. As Thomas suggested with his story of the Muslims and the Christians, individuals are interdependent.

In another twist, neo-conservatives who do acknowledge interdependence often cite it to justify their policies. Since one action affects others, a tax cut for the middle class will produce spin-offs that trickle down to the poor. Without empathy, however, a middle-class family has no self-interest in seeing others benefit from its newfound fortune. Saving money therefore becomes as compelling a choice as spending it. Personal renewal can amount to nothing more than personal enrichment, leaving a homeless family still scraping food from a dumpster.

Neo-conservatives, it should be said, have a version of empathy called tough love. By that logic, far from deterring personal renewal, homelessness could kickstart it. Sometimes, after all, the prospect of hustling food from the floor of a garbage bin is the only incentive to change from within and retaste the fruits of self-sufficiency. As a result, cutting people off welfare is the "most compassionate" way to break the "cycle of dependency," set lost souls back on course and thus empower ordinary folks.

Here is a world view motivated not by meanness but by thoughtlessness. Conveniently neglecting their own pumped rhetoric of pulling oneself up by the bootstraps, luminaries of the new Right kneel at the altar of rigid ideology and invest faith that whatever happens should happen. This ritual approaches gutlessness, because it abdicates control after the initial act of cutting. Where starry-eyed neo-cons espouse ritualistic responsibility, empathy demands rational responsibility. It calls on us to think, in every action, about how much consideration we owe the other. Empathy arises, in Thomas's words, out of "self-questioning."

For him and his fellow activists, self-questioning departs wildly from indulging in "rights talk." According to philosopher Richard Rorty, exclusive reliance on the language of rights only serves to issue "unconditional commands"; it does not explain to people why they should care enough to listen. "Instead of saying, for example, that the absence of various legal protections makes the lives of homosexuals unbearably difficult, that it creates unnecessary human suffering for our fellow [citizens]," Rorty laments, progressive people "have come to say that these protections must be instituted in order to protect homosexuals' rights." Which then clears the path for assorted opponents to hold up the constitution and accurately proclaim that it contains no defence of bestiality, pedophilia and other presumed gay rights. In the interests of securing proper rights, not reinforcing mythical ones, Rorty urges each of us to question our role in distracting from "what is really needed in this case: an attempt by the straights to put themselves in the shoes of gays." His is a plea for empathy not only among conservatives but more immediately among progressives.

To be sure, things get decidedly more complicated when we ask: Empathize with whom? Everyone? I do not think so. Thomas, for example, feels no compulsion to walk in the boots of the Montreal police, but neither does he demonize them. By the same token, he tries to understand why many men of colour resort to sexism and homophobia without brushing off their behaviour as harmless. In short, we can be empathetic towards stockbrokers and not just single parents, Muslims and not just Christians, by acknowledging their common humanity. But the troubles of a stockbroker will not keep me awake at night; the more pressing plight of a single parent might.

Thinking people make these types of distinctions all the time. We discriminate rationally. When confronted by a panhandler, I decide whether to give based on a hastily configured hierarchy—old before young, non-smokers before smokers, those with well-worn no-names before those with scuffed-up Nikes. I can never be sure I am giving to the "right" people. But empathy reminds me that the same risk afflicts panhandlers. They can never be sure they are approaching the "right" people—folks who will not preach, spit, yell or curse at them. Yet panhandlers will get burned more often than I will. At twenty-five or fifty cents, mine is a pretty cheap risk. Not so for most panhandlers. The consequences of being burned are significantly heavier for them than for me, because they have fewer choices.

So I can choose to revile the appearance of panhandlers and, in erecting that wall, deny any similarity in our situations. Or I can choose to focus on our common dilemma. By remembering that I am not the only one with an ethical predicament—to ask or not to ask for loose change is as much a predicament as to give or not to give—I relate to panhandlers in a way that tells me, "There go I. Now what am I going to do about it?" And if I do not know what to do about it, at least I can look them in the eye. Their connection to my world will not have gone unnoticed by me.

Empathy is a reality check. It forces us to figure out, then face, our responsibilities.

Twenty-seven-year-old Trudy Parsons accepts personal responsibility for contracting HIV, the virus linked to AIDS. In turn, she wants politicians and public health officials to share responsibility for removing the stigma that surrounds HIV. It is a stigma to which I succumbed: while staying at Trudy's apartment in St. John's, Newfoundland, I placed my head on her pillow, brushed my teeth over her bathroom sink, drank tea from her mugs, stirred milk with her spoons, and more than once had to console my queasy gut that "I can't get it this way."

At age twenty, Trudy contracted HIV from only her third sex partner ever. He did not use a condom. She did not know that you do not necessarily get infected on the first unprotected fuck, so she figured there was no point in pushing a condom on him after that. Following bouts of the flu, rashes and mouth infections, Trudy suspected she had HIV. But every time she booked a blood test, she backed out. Even volunteering with an AIDS organization months later could not bring Trudy to confirm her own status. Finally, an unexpected call from a health official led to her diagnosis.

In a dilemma that translates into dark comedy, Trudy wanted to commit suicide, yet worried about infecting whomever found her body. "I didn't realize that HIV dies on contact with air," she remembers. "So there I was, feeling like a complete asshole. I couldn't keep myself from getting HIV, I have horrible taste in men and I can't even commit suicide right. My gosh! And now I have to live. It was terrible." By necessity, the private denial dissipated; the public activism began.

At the time of my visit, Trudy was coordinator of women's programs at the Newfoundland and Labrador AIDS Committee, a contract position whose federal funding has since evaporated. But, sounding healthy on the phone, she recently told me that she still takes on projects for the committee. To get there, Trudy had to fight her former employer, a national home-care company whose clients include people with HIV and AIDS. Upon hearing of her condition, the company fired Trudy. "They called me after my [twelve-hour] shift and asked if I would come into the office. When I got down there, the company claimed that they got an anonymous phone call saying that I'd tested positive for HIV and was this true? Nobody knew about this, hardly, so the 'yes' kind of got stuck in my throat." Two weeks later—three days before Christmas—the company terminated her employment under Newfoundland's Home Care and Day Services Regulations. "Mind you, they were really nice about it," Trudy reports of the company's local office; she suspects the axe swung down from headquarters in Ontario.

Trudy then arrived at a difficult decision. Recognizing that she "had to nip injustice in the bud, otherwise I'd let people walk all over me for the rest of my life," she took the company to the provincial human rights commission. Had a fevered vindication of rights and a handsome payment been her agenda, Trudy could have hired a lawyer and gone to court. But even in hindsight, she accepts that her rights are tempered by everyone else's. "I really wanted to be fair about all of this," Trudy says of her decision not to litigate. The human rights commission did not exactly help on the fairness front: at one point in the drawn-out case, mediators asked her to settle for $1500. She refused, reminding them that her battle was about more than an individual's compensation; it was about medical accuracy, government policy and a community's dignity. A year later, Trudy won. Her victory put the province on notice to amend the Home Care and Day Services Regulations, allowing people with HIV to be employed in that field. Five years and no amendment later, a provincial official tells me that "a new draft of the legislation is under review, and change is on the way."

Trudy's successive struggles with the company, the commission and the government were fuelled by an abiding empathy with the women of Newfoundland. "There are more women, per capita, getting infected in this province than anywhere else in the country," Trudy notes. "That's for a whole series of reasons. Violence against women, especially in the rural parts. If you haven't been battered by your husband or boyfriend by the time you're seventeen, there's something wrong with ya!" Unemployment, illiteracy, Catholicism, the lack of women's centres and the self-deprecating culture of Newfoundland, which reinforces the low self-esteem of people—"all of that needs to be confronted," Trudy states.

With so much to take on in the province she calls home, Trudy turned down job offers from outside Newfoundland at twice the meagre salary she earned at the AIDS committee. Her empathy for the women of her province has sometimes been reciprocated. "I'll never forget being at a women's centre in Labrador, and it was the first time that I'd ever gone to a community where I felt like a 'member of' and not a 'visitor to.' They asked me about the costs of living with HIV and AIDS, and I mentioned that some people I know are spending $2500 a month on treatment. They wanted to know how much I spent, so I told them about a regular prescription I get, which costs $140 for three days. Well, I walked out of that women's centre with money for my next prescription. It was embarrassing but incredibly sweet." She recalls thinking: "It wouldn't be bad to test positive in this city. It really wouldn't. Hail the female Labradorians!"

Still, empathy from neighbours has not always been forthcoming. Voices on the other end of her mother's phone line have claimed that her daughter, the whore, got what she deserved. Trudy has also received hate mail and found, tacked to her apartment door, death threats that police suspect were scrawled by an acquaintance or friend. "I don't walk the streets at all any more," Trudy admits. "Regardless of what strangers come up and say to me, it's hard always being 'that woman with AIDS.' I want my time out. I need to be a person before my HIV status, not my HIV status and then a person."

The unwelcome scrutiny has forced her to reexamine various shibboleths of womanhood. Trudy once "did the feminine thing"—big hair, cute clothes—so that people would listen to her. On balance, they did not. Then she took to hiding under more garb. "Since I was known for my really long, curly hair, I started wearing all of these hats, hoping that people wouldn't recognize me. That helped for a while but then I got known for the hats. It drove me crazy." At the same time, she felt uncomfortable with her appearance because she was living a female stereotype. "If I looked sweet and unthreatening enough, life would be hunky-dory." She guffaws. "Right!"

Eventually, Trudy tossed out all the signs of feigned femininity, going the whole nine yards. When she picked me up from the St. John's airport, she sported a shaven head, stretch pants revealing a good portion of her prickly legs and a button announcing "Hate is not a family value." "Hair?" she shrugs. "Big deal. Got rid of it. Except on my legs and armpits. If hair grows there, let it be. It takes so long to shave when I could be doing more important things." She also swore off make-up. "A lot of people think that's because I'm feeling really bad about myself. Actually, I feel great now that I'm being me."

In another move to save self-respect, Trudy has almost entirely stopped talking to the media. Its fixation on image romanticizes HIV and AIDS. A 1993 feature in *Maclean's*, Canada's national news magazine, described Trudy as being "[o]f slender build, with a mane of thick black hair framing her thin, serious face." She rolls her eyes as she recites from the page. "Do I sound like a desperate, lonely waif?" she blurts. The last thing Trudy does before we leave each other in St. John's is hand me a thoroughly marked-up version of that article. "I've underlined all the places where they romanticized me," she informs. I take the hint.

What Trudy hopes for is a media that closes the distance between itself and the world it chronicles, journalists who understand that empathy can serve the cause of accuracy. "One reporter, when he first saw me, said, 'You don't look sick enough.' Sick enough for what? Public pity? Good ratings? It's important that we see people in their final stages, but what about the reality that people live with HIV for many, many years and do different things in that time span?" More a believer in idiocy than in conspiracy, Trudy nonetheless wonders if media stereotyping "is a way for people to keep themselves separate from the 'likes of us,' so HIV doesn't have to be their issue, too. As long as the media talk *about* us, rather than talk *with* us, we're studies, tragic victims who can be plunked on pedestals and pitied. But I don't want to be outside on a pedestal. I want to be inside on an equal footing."

Trudy gets dismissive reactions not just from the usual sources but also from flag-bearers in the HIV/AIDS movement, primarily gay men who have politicized the issue and often do not notice when women get lost in the shuffle. Trudy illustrates. "At a national conference, a friend and I were raising some issues around women and AIDS and one man got very impatient and said, 'Yeah, okay, enough about women involved in the movement.' I said, 'Excuse me, it's women *infected* and involved.' If he wants HIV to be a gay male disease, it can be in his world. But not in mine. And not in the real world."

She has witnessed enough separating and dividing to rattle off a predictable pattern to the splits. "There's a division among people about how you contracted HIV. There's the IV drug users, there's the hemophiliacs, there's the gay men, there's the straight women, there's the lesbian IV drug users, there's the bisexuals." Trudy reconsiders. "Actually, no, bisexuals don't fit in anywhere at all. We'll just put 'them' on another planet and 'they' can deal with 'their' issues. That's the attitude." Differences matter, she affirms, but that is exactly why empathy should, too. "Having differences doesn't mean we can't all be involved in the process of understanding the issues and giving some input. I want to know what gay men are doing, I really do. I think they've done amazing work. I want to further that, honour and respect that."

Openness has taught Trudy to question her own simmering prejudices, including the assumption that behind every gay man with AIDS is a sexual act. "I met a gay man who was seventeen and having a horrible time coming to terms with his sexual orientation. He just didn't know how he'd fit into the world. So he started using drugs, and eventually started shooting drugs, and that's how he contracted HIV. We always assume that gay men get it from anal sex, but here's a guy who never had anal sex. He got HIV, you could say, from homophobia." She has also met gay hemophiliacs who acquired HIV from tainted blood.

If Trudy's empathy starts with openness, it stops short of nosiness. "I don't ask people their sexual orientation any more, never ask them how long they've been HIV positive and never ask how they got it. Taking away those three things means that I can't make quickie judgements. The information will inevitably come out in conversation, so when I do judge someone, it's by what I hear them say or see them do, not what I *assume* they're about. If you're saying something that I think is really strange, or fuck awful, or wonderful, we can go from there." Echoing Thomas Ponniah, she is convinced that "I learn something from everybody."

Having been moved beyond her own assumptions, Trudy knows it is not inconceivable to do the same with Newfoundland's legislators, doctors and bureaucrats. The "old farts" among them do not thwart her vision of a society that empowers the individual by trusting his or her capacity to make informed decisions once that information has been shared. "When people go in for testing, I would like to see them get a little package about what this means, what's happening, what the laws are. It has to be written so that people can understand. Literacy rights are important anywhere, but in this province they could be the difference between life and death."

Those diagnosed with HIV should then have the tools to disclose their status with dignity, she says. "Right now, all they're really given is a lecture—or, if they infect someone, a prison sentence. That's no way to stop the epidemic; it doesn't give people healthy choices. You get safer sex pamphlets geared at the non-infected community but never at the HIV-positive community. It's not, 'Here's what you do to protect others *and* your own esteem after you've contracted HIV.' Our society terrorizes people into respecting others instead of teaching them about self-respect first."

Trudy's message of self-help through social understanding should appeal to conservatives and progressives alike, but there is still that minor irritant of fear. If even I could not deny my trepidation as I ate from Trudy's plates and touched her toilet seat, then how would she persuade those with antithetical convictions to let down their guard? In a province socialized by the Church, how does she educate people to "be not afraid"?

Trudy's secret ammunition is humour. "You know what HIV stands for? Humour Is Vital. Almost everyone I know who's been in the movement awhile is hysterically funny because people can say such strange things to you after you're diagnosed that if you can't laugh, you'll just crack, go insane and die." She says that students at Catholic schools, with whom she often speaks, appreciate her departure from monotone sermonizing. She used to follow the instructions of the Christian Brothers and attempt solemnity, but that took all the fun out of fighting HIV. Fun? I ask. "A young woman asked me how I dispose of my tampons," Trudy relates. "I told her, kidding of course, that I mail them to all the people I don't like. I said that to break the ice because she was really nervous to have asked about this in a group of her peers. I thought it was a brilliant question that deserved a moment of lightness."

To be sure, Trudy nods, "some schools get really mad at me for offering choices. I'm a feminist, though. I'm not a terrorist. If people are consumed by tears, they can't be activated." A handful of young women walked into one workshop with boxes of tissues. "I told them, 'Girlfriends, you're not going to need these.' And they were amazed, thrilled, that they didn't end up using them. Instead of being busy wallowing in despair, they knew there were other things they could do."

In more than one sense, Trudy's humour is vital—vital meaning crucial, but also meaning kinetic, energizing, action-inducing. By recognizing people's fears for the sake of mobilizing their spirits, Trudy connects empathy to agency.

Where empathy renders us human, agency is a value that gets to the core of what makes us human *beings*. A woman in a wheelchair, twenty-four-year-old Nicole Soucey, embodies that set of possibilities.

CHAPTER 6

agency

The first thing I notice about Nicole Soucey is that she is short; four feet two inches to be precise. The low counters in her apartment in Vanier, a suburb of Ottawa, and her specially fitted car, with its extra-long gear shift, big seats and prominent pedals, hammer home the fact that equality cannot mean treating everyone "the same."

Nicole was born with arthrogryposis, a shrinkage of muscle and tendon tissue that restricts the movement of her joints. Her first operation reconstructed a flat skull to relieve pressure on the brain. Then a hole in the ceiling of her mouth had to be looked after. As a fifth-grader, she went back into the hospital to have a curved spine corrected. But Nicole is more than the sum of her nine surgeries, which raises the second thing I notice about her.

She has wit. In a biting barb aimed at the way some activists manipulate identity politics, Nicole summarizes what it is to be a woman with a disability, a bisexual and a francophone. "It's like winning Lotto 6/49." Then she chortles, lifting her arms in mock victory.

Sometimes, when people stare at Nicole in her wheelchair, she hops out, stands up and yells, "It's a miracle!" "I find it funny to see their faces drop," she confesses. Especially at the gas station. "People expect to see somebody tall and instead this shorty comes out of the car. So I smile and give a big wave." Like Trudy Parsons, Nicole wields humour as a tool of change because anger relaxes neither individuals nor the tension of a situation. But relaxation can beget complacency. Nicole's humour sometimes conspires with her basic mobility to make her appear so empowered that people forget she has special needs.

Her cheekiness is always accompanied by a more serious approach. To build support for accessibility, Nicole invites people into her wheelchair. "They see how frustrating it is when the only obstacle in their path is a step that's not even the height of a hundred-page book." To demystify the pain of homophobia, Nicole sometimes challenges heterosexuals to "have a conversation about their partners without saying 'he' or 'she,' as if they're not out as a couple." Being closeted, they soon learn, "is a hell of a task." As well, "when your first language is French," as hers is, "to have to speak English at a social service office that advertises as bilingual but actually has one French-speaking counsellor with a really long waiting list—and I'm talking about an official language of the country—I would love for anglophones to try it." (In a sense, Afra Jalabi did—and understands better than ever francophone frustration.)

Nicole's point is, if people do not understand where she is coming from they often will not care where she needs to be. If they do not care, they are not motivated to help her get there. And if they empathize but still do not sympathize, Nicole says she will have lost nothing by invoking her agency and making the effort to reach them. "I'm glad I'm assertive and good-humoured enough to pull a few people into my wheelchair," she grins. "That way, I can kick them out too." Which brings me to the third thing I notice.

Nicole is a strategist extraordinaire. She divides her political activism between Pink Triangle Youth (PTY), a grassroots service organization for gays, lesbians and bisexuals, and the feminist DisAbled Women's Network (DAWN). But for her, agency cannot be as black and white as joining a protest. Because she is able-bodied enough to get out of her wheelchair and manoeuvre a car, and because she can be attracted to women as well as men, and because she can switch from French to English, she is constantly navigating the grey zone of popular prejudices. That takes negotiating skill. So, rather than carp endlessly about what has not happened, part of her strategy is to keep ambivalent allies onside by thanking people whose attitudes are improving.

Including devout Catholics. "My mom still thinks that when I go to PTY meetings, I'm there to watch pornos," Nicole admits. "But I have to acknowledge all of the little things that she does right." For instance, as a fan of religious TV, her mother taped a Church-sponsored program about homosexuality and asked Nicole to watch it with her. No preview of purgatory ensued. "I was amazed at how positive the show was," says Nicole. "My mom and I talked about it afterwards and I just let her know how thankful I was that she thought of me."

Nicole so appreciates negotiation that she will not stand in almighty judgement of her mother's coping methods, even when they clash with her own. "It's hard being out to my mom because I don't want her to lose the image of me as her innocent little girl. This image has been her way of getting through all the hardships around my disability, and I have to be sensitive to that. When I had my operations, I know my mother was in the waiting room crying her eyes out because she couldn't do anything for me. If she could've been in my shoes, she would've."

It is when her mother's love degenerates into pity that Nicole draws the line. "I challenge her. When we go to a public place and my mom sees someone in a wheelchair, she says, 'Oh, that poor soul.' And I'm like, 'Mom, she has a life! Maybe she'd rather be walking but being in a wheelchair doesn't have to be a barrier to her happiness.' "

Despite resigning herself to the reality that her parents will always see her as their "special baby," Nicole holds fast to the most obvious yet most often overlooked trick of communication: understand the other person. "People can't change overnight. You have to take it day by day, communicating, not letting them off the hook too easily. Most of all, you have to be patient."

By heeding those words, Nicole has made sure her disability does not overwhelm the possibility of a career. While attending college, she accepted that her physical needs would restrict choices such as acting, a passion from which able-bodied people have a hard enough time squeezing a living. Nicole shuddered at the thought of being a bored secretary, and did not want to teach school as her mother had. Friends told her she listened well, so she decided to study social work. A recent graduate of that field, Nicole has since landed a part-time job at a resource centre for disabled persons. Here, she dispenses advice on everything from building renovations to counselling methods. Knowing the need both for a competitive edge and for a sense of community, Nicole gains other social work experience from volunteerism—which tests her patience, and command of communication, like nothing else.

Particularly her dealings with self-anointed emancipators. "In the gay and lesbian community, there's a big myth that because you're disabled, you're asexual," Nicole groans. "There's also a myth about bisexuality: that you're sitting on the fence and temporarily confused." She points out that her mother has harboured similar prejudices about gays ("they're just finding out who they are"), raising questions about how these homosexists can claim to be more liberated than the supposed homophobes they slam. "I've got the capacity to care for both sexes, for a *person*," Nicole emphasizes. "I don't want to care for a shell. Like in religion, they say that when you go on to the next life, you won't have the body, but the spirit. I try to look at the spirit of the person."

The trouble is, others do not look back, or around, or down. "A lot of times at PTY meetings, people will say good-bye to me verbally and then they'll turn to a person who's nearby and they'll start giving hugs. Hello! Over here, please! It may not be convenient for a six-foot-tall person to bend down two feet, but if you ask me, I'll tell you that I need hugs like everybody else."

A missed hug will not shatter anyone, least of all Nicole. Still, unless people become alert—unless they acknowledge their own agency in matters big and little—an embrace denied today can balloon into a more profound invisibility tomorrow. Nicole considered quitting PTY when she discovered that its office would be moved to an inaccessible location. Only then was another woman in the group stirred to action; she worried that once Nicole pulled out, PTY would be made up almost completely of men. An understandable, if jarring, self-interest born of the odd politics behind representation.

When the fellow member belatedly asked her to help PTY find an accessible address, Nicole did not dwell on her feelings of annoyance. She, too, invoked self-interest. "I knew that nobody else in the group could do it better than me, so I was happy to get involved and have the job done properly." After the move, for instance, PTY's pamphlet had to be revised. The first draft neglected to mention that the new location was wheelchair accessible. "I immediately told the coordinator, who looked at me like, 'Another problem?' " Nicole remembers. "But I was there to get the job done right." (In the end, she says, PTY opted to replace floppy pamphlets with more discreet business-style cards. Their size does not allow for information about accessibility.)

Considering the routine disappointments, I am not surprised to hear many disability rights militants argue that it is not their responsibility to educate everyone else. But, in talking to Nicole, I realize that this line only contributes to the bane of progressive activism in the last decade. The scandal of so much identity politics is that it does not advise people to recognize when they have power; rather, it cajoles people simply to demand that they be handed power. Nicole warns that this approach can unduly quash personal agency and collective empowerment. "Let's get real," she urges. "If you want something to happen from your perspective, then it's in your interest, regardless of whether or not it's your responsibility, to educate others. In the long run, the people you've educated will be able to teach someone else. For me, being an effective activist is all about being practical."

How practical? "You not only have to know how to speak up; you have to know how to shut up. And listen. Just listen. In life, you've got to learn to give and take, right? That's why communication is so vital to our society. If I say, 'I deserve this on the spot, it's your duty, you're obliged to give me this right,' chances are that people will get defensive. But if I say, 'Is there some way we can compromise so that you have your dignity and I have mine?' then what I'm really compromising is the strategy, not the result."

She pulls out the example of a restaurant in which the bathrooms are fifteen steps up. "I can say right off the bat that the owners are not inhuman, okay? They might have tried putting the bathrooms closer to ground level but were screwed [around] by building codes and overly picky bureaucrats. They might not have the money for all the renovations. I mean, proper facilities can cost a lot, and even restaurant owners have to live and pay for things outside of their restaurant. So, I'd try to reach a deal with the owners: They look into building one accessible washroom on the ground floor. In the meantime, I'm going to go to the bathroom before I come to their restaurant."

Suppose you have to go to the bathroom every two hours? "Well, they can serve me faster than their other customers so I can be out of there in two hours. They can also find out for me where there's an accessible washroom in a building close by." Likening an understanding of her disability to somebody else's food allergies, she says that whether it is a bathroom or a list of ingredients, "everybody has to make their needs known, and frankly, I need a nice, relaxing evening out more than I need a screaming match with someone."

Those tempted to accuse Nicole of underestimating confrontation, of being so generous with civility that she opens herself up to exploitation, have missed the essence of agency: It is the willingness to recognize our own power to help get the job done. I cannot be aware of my power without a sense of my limits. Conserving my energy for a greater battle is as much a decision arising from agency as is squaring my jaw and venturing forth.

Nicole epitomizes personal power not simply by defining her limits but also by making the most of her limited circumstances: responding to instead of retreating from strangers' stares, her mother's pity, the gay community's complacency. Forever negotiating, she takes ownership of problems. Somebody has to, and protracted bickering about whose responsibility it is will not get the job done. Such bickering forfeits personal power to the seductions of group resentment. What limp, dumb defeats those are.

My conception here of personal power—of agency—should not be confused with the cult of individualism championed by the new Right. Neo-conservatives treat personal power as a wedge, suggesting that individual initiative can and should prevent group action. In particular, they have sold North America's middle class an impression of personal power that addresses the individual taxpayer and assures her that she does have power, if only the government and special interest groups would not rob her of it.

How has the old Left answered? Personal power is a capitalist hoax; without socialism, we are slaves to the System. Witness the assumptions with which York University political scientist James Laxer begins his 1996 book *In Search of a New Left*. He wastes no time telling us that those who have been privatized out of jobs "will *never* work again. These believers in the system that *destroyed* them are *condemned* to a slow loss of self-esteem, a waning of respect from family and friends." (Emphasis mine.) By defining individuals strictly as workers, Laxer presumes our complete annihilation in the face of unemployment. Having gone through it a few times now, I can attest that unemployment is unpleasant. But I choose to give it the perspective that Michael Ignatieff suggests: we all spin multiple identities from our web of multiple relations. I, and quite possibly Nicole, would be more "destroyed" if we lost our mothers than our contracts, because a lifetime of negotiating our identities as daughters can take precedence over our fleeting functions as employees. I think his fascination with the idea of renewed class warfare is one of the reasons that Laxer, a commandant of the old Left, has failed to find the new Left that he claims to seek.

Hence the extent of the fundamentalist vision: the Right zings a positive message about the personal power of the taxpayer; the Left lobs back a negative message about the powerlessness of the individual worker. Both camps are ensnared in an either/or mentality. To believe that individual agency precludes community empowerment is to believe that every man, woman and child is an island. As has already been demonstrated, we are interdependent. If empathy grounds us, and agency drives us, then our lives are inseverable from all the conditions around us, so that we can affect everyone we touch.

Even the seemingly obstinate: despite wondering what kinky things Nicole does at those PTY meetings, her mother has been moved enough by her daughter's openness to voluntarily view a program on homosexuality, then invite Nicole to watch it with her *again*. Likewise, the process by which we become ourselves is shaped, directly and indirectly, by myriad others—and in not-so-obvious ways. Nicole has imbibed a part of her mother's religious teachings, extending the Catholic reverence for spirit into a defence of her own bisexuality.

Agency, then, is about human *being*—thinking, doing, strategizing, changing. When asked to name her most outrageous deed as an activist, Trudy Parsons answered, "Living. I wish that every person diagnosed with HIV was out. My little political mind says, 'Yes, we should all be out' and my humane side says, 'That's not possible.' But I really think people have to speak for themselves. The biggest thing we could ever do, if we want to make changes, is to be in front of those changes, just living."

Half a continent to the west, Karen Pederson pushes the frontier of another way of life. At twenty-two, she is thinking of taking over her family's stead, a honey-making business in Cutknife, Saskatchewan. Clue number one that she has earned some respect from nature: "The bees were really cranky on a particular day two months ago, maybe because it was raining. As soon as I opened the hive, they rushed out at me. I backed up and got ten, fifteen stings on my face. I haven't worked in the field that long but I must have developed an immunity by that point because I wound up with only one puff on my temple."

Besides taking her lumps, Karen has paid her dues in beads of sweat.

Having been youth president of the National Farmers' Union (NFU), Canada's most outspoken advocate of rural families, she knows how tough it is to sell the farm to young people, literally and figuratively. The hard hat she wears confirms that breeding and branding queen bees can rattle the nerves. But, cropping from her grandfather's bee-keeping hobby, the honey-making focus of the Pederson farm has grown along with Karen. Slightly embarrassed, she shows me photos of herself diaper-clad in the bee yards. At age nine, Karen began to devote set hours to the assembly-line chore of extracting honey from heavy combs in a sweltering, sickeningly sweet–smelling shack. (During harvest season, which coincides with the stagnant heat of summer, workdays stretch from 8:00 a.m. to 6:00 p.m.) In her mid-teens, she taught farm workers how to operate the extractor, eventually managing anywhere from three full-timers throughout the year to nine at harvest. Most recently, she graduated to supervise the scarier process of stripping honey from the hives themselves. All that experience has rendered Karen "the rover"—the person who can take on any farm job, be it lugging sixty-pound boxes or meticulously monitoring combs for queen bees. To run the farm, she figures, "I'll need the credibility that says I've earned my right to be here."

Belonging cannot be too airy-fairy a concern for Karen, because farm culture is rife with double standards for women. These are the roots of her pragmatic feminism, a philosophy that sustains her personal struggle to be accepted as a farmer, not belittled as "the wife" or "the gopher." Although feminist organizing claims a proud tradition on the Canadian Prairies, advancing the causes of medicare, voluntary birth control and the vote, farm women are still waiting for their contributions to be adequately counted. Today, off-farm jobs held mostly by women keep family farms afloat, yet only a slim percentage of those farms have legal partnership agreements between husband and wife. At its tenth anniversary celebration, the Alberta Women in Support of Agriculture presented eight men and one woman as speakers. Asks Karen, "How will women ever convince men that we're just as expert in farming as they are if we don't change the way we look at ourselves?"

She has certainly had to. "Even though I started quite young, only now do I see myself as a farmer and not just an employee," Karen admits. "But some of my friends who drive grain trucks for their dads don't realize that technically they're farming. Even my mom, when she takes meals out to the field at harvest time, she's helping to keep the combines going. Folks don't tend to view those extra jobs as part of farming because they don't view the *whole* farm. As farming becomes more of a business, they consider only the money-making part as legitimate."

As such, she will play the dollars game. But some of the moves will be her own. "Bankers, machine dealers and people like that — they'll want my business when I'm running the farm. If I give them the message that 'You have to take me seriously; I'm not going to take any flak from you,' then they'll have no choice because my farm is as much their business as mine. You have to be confident in your own place here so others realize you're not asking for that place; you already have it. It's a matter of me sending that signal clearly."

Karen's confidence comes, in part, from her participation in the NFU. A long-time progressive organization with links to international "peasant movements" (as distinct from corporate farms), the NFU is where Karen's parents met, where they put her in daycare and where she got involved in the intrigues of policy-making at age twelve. By taking up the key issue of food security, the NFU helps to ensure that people can properly feed themselves through safe production, fair marketing and accessible distribution. With that in mind, Karen protested at a recent Saskatoon visit by Prime Minister Jean Chrétien, challenging him to reread his 1993 election platform, the Red Book. She also attended the 1995 Beijing world women's conference as an agricultural delegate. Meeting only two other such delegates reminded Karen to appreciate the leadership of women in the NFU. "Walking the picket line, going to conferences, participating in foreign exchanges, giving talks, representing the union—it can't but be noticed that women are right there," she says.

On occasion, however, she has had to assert her own agency, even against the kind of union guy who hollers slogans of solidarity on the picket line. "There was one NFU prep session for people going on an exchange trip to the Caribbean," she recalls. "A fortyish man from Alberta was discussing farming with some of the Caribbeans and wanted to compare Saskatchewan and Alberta. So he looked around and asked, 'Are there any guys from Saskatchewan?' He really did mean guys. Three Saskatchewan women were around but he completely ignored us. I said to him, 'You have an image problem about who can be a farmer.' I try not to be too antagonistic when I'm doing these things just because it seems to work better that way. You catch them when they've actually done something, so they can't argue with you about what you saw! Well, he reacted by not saying another word. That was his contribution to recognizing the role of women in agriculture." This strategist believes in a certain subtlety.

Other situations, though, call for persistence more than subtlety. "While I was on an exchange trip to Denmark, I lived with a farming family for several months. I quite regularly asked about farm politics and government policies because that was part of my reason for being there, right? The farmer never came out and said, 'You're a woman, you wouldn't understand these things.' It was more like, 'Well, you don't need to know this …' His hired hand was fresh out of agriculture school and basically had no farming experience. He didn't even come from a farm. But the way this farmer would talk to the two of us—I was way down and he was right up there. Towards the end of my stay, the farmer got the point that I wanted information even if he wouldn't take the time to explain things to me.

"One morning, he was reading the paper and came across an article about the Progressive Conservative leadership race in Canada—the race to replace [Prime Minister Brian] Mulroney. [The farmer] thought he'd tell me because he knew I was interested in politics. So I asked, 'Does it say who's running?' He listed off all these names, and when he got down to Kim Campbell, the farmer quite obviously said 'he.' I said, 'No, she's a woman.' We had this argument about whether she's a woman or a man because Kim is a man's name in Denmark." She adds with a grin, "This guy thought I was out of my tree."

So did a male employee back home on the Pederson farm. He told "the boss," Mr. Pederson, that he could not take orders from a young woman. Replied Mr. Pederson: "If she gives you the order that you're fired, you are." Karen let the worker think about it. He stayed on.

Her mother and father never doubted Karen, and therein lie the seeds of her agency. "When my parents took me to the NFU picket line at age six, they would, to the best of their ability, explain why we were doing this. When I decided to travel after high school, my parents were completely behind me even though some of my teachers thought, 'Go to university right away, otherwise you'll never make use of your intelligence.' They didn't see that travelling and farming are as much a use of my brain as a classroom education. Now I can think about running the farm partly because my parents always trusted me to make decisions and held me responsible for them. Without their respect, I wouldn't have that choice."

Nor would Karen have what she terms the "one value that will guide me throughout life: respect for all, total domination for none." She says this not only as a feminist but also as a farmer. "For instance, you've got sandy soil and rocky soil. To bring out their best qualities, you have to recognize that the sandy soil may have something so different to it that you can't treat it like the rocky soil. Both are good pieces of land, but you have to take into account their differences if you're going to give them equal respect." It is the same with her feminism, she says. "My feminism is that if I want to be in a traditionally male job—construction or farming—I can, and if my brother wants to be a nurse, he can. But I also believe that women and men are innately different so we shouldn't have to be exactly like each other. As long as I'm good at what I do, my differences should be respected. They might even make the results better."

Fusing empathy and agency, Karen defines respect as "making the effort to learn distinctions instead of just assuming." Example: Reminiscent of Tzeporah Berman's image of the She-Logger from Hell, a friend of Karen's once reacted to her as a horned agent from Planet T-Bone. Objecting to the way meat is often produced in the U.S., yet having researched nothing about Canadian farming techniques, this friend became vegetarian. "I have nothing against vegetarians," Karen says, "but people should understand that farm animals aren't treated cruelly everywhere." She distinguishes between family farms and corporate farms. "On family farms, you have probably one or two hundred animals. We grow pretty attached to the animals because we're dealing with them every day, so only a sick farmer would take pleasure in seeing them suffer." On corporate farms, "the managers are looking strictly at profit-and-loss statements, so there's just no connection between human and animal." Thus, Karen concludes, it seems respectful of both people and animals to defend family farms. "Multinationals would love to close family farms all over the world and use the land for more 'gainful' purposes. Let the small farm die and you're taking away one more element of social justice."

The tapestry she is stitching brings out the interdependence of all creatures; social justice starts with seeing this mutuality. "You can't separate men and women, or respect for children and respect for nature, or the survival of medicare and the survival of farming communities." I tell her that these platitudes sound pleasing, but what do they really mean? "It's like the globe—you've got different continents but they're not necessarily separated. There's still all that land and water connecting them. Women's issues, race issues, the environment, farming: it's one huge sphere and you've got to constantly bear those other parts in mind." And if you do not? "If you have the blinders on, and you can't see the rest of the world, how will you know whether your position in it is getting better or worse? How will you know that you're even on the same planet?"

If empathy requires looking outside ourselves to put the peripheral into perspective, then agency compels us to ask: What will we do with our newfound bigger picture?

Dana Putnam changed after sighting her bigger picture. The grand-daughter of a teacher and daughter of a self-educated single mother, she grew up in "borderline poverty" and hopes to do literacy work in struggling communities. Her partner of thirteen years, Dan, is a self-employed carpenter who dabbles in music and earns a pay cheque that is seasonal at best, sporadic usually. They have an eight-year-old daughter, Sylvia. Home is a bungalow stalwartly situated on the edge of Vancouver, along the industrial arm of the Fraser River, in a neighbourhood that also features a sprawling network of condos. But life inside that bungalow gives thirty-year-old Dana an understanding of change which might not have come from her childhood sometimes spent in "communal houses, with alternative music by women." To challenge the real world, Dana has had to be *in* it.

"Very soon after I had Sylvia," she remembers, "something hit me. All of a sudden I was a mother and sort of a wife. When I told people I was having a hard time, they'd either pat me on the back because I've 'done the womanly thing' or they'd look at me like, 'What's wrong with you? Women have had babies for millennia.' Dan was working nights, so when he was home, he slept, and the baby and I needed to be quiet. He withdrew because he was going through his own freaked-out/bummed-out thing. But he could get away with it; I couldn't."

She wound up at a postpartum depression group, "which was the beginning of me recognizing that, hey, this isn't just *my* inadequacy; it's all the myths of motherhood—the TV ads, the social expectations. Anybody living a myth would be overwhelmed."

Dana now lives a question instead of a myth: "How does my reality fit with my ideals as a feminist?" Having partially replaced "the mainstream-way-to-do-things tape in my head," she has managed to come up with a few solutions to the long-standing conundrum of being a homemaker without being a door mat.

"When I go to do the dishes, for instance, I'm thinking division of labour. Like, 'Why am I doing these for the fourth night in a row?' I simply say to Dan, 'You expect me to wash these?' I prefer those sorts of challenges because telling him point blank takes responsibility off of him to learn when it's his turn to contribute to the household."

Ever vigilant of the tape in her head, Dana catches her presumptions midstream. "I have to say that my standard of [domestic equality] isn't the only standard. It's not like I sit Dan down and drill feminism into him. It's more like, he's giving me room to approach things differently. That's what people who care about each other do: clear out space to try new things and hopefully learn from each other along the way."

As Dana and Dan educate each other, a second relationship benefits—the one between parent and child. Dan now pays attention to Sylvia's intake of TV violence, insisting as well that her toy collection exclude guns and knives. Dana's chief concern for her daugher is body image. "At a year and a half, Sylvia said, 'Mommy, I'm fat.' At such a young age, she saw 'fat' as something to be ashamed of, something 'abnormal.' So we talk a lot." But reasoning even with a child demands a strategy. For example, Dana often waits to debunk a stereotype for Sylvia because, she believes, "it puts someone on the defensive to contradict them right away." Especially in ambiguous areas like sexuality. "Only a couple of months ago [Sylvia] said, 'Girls can't get married to girls and boys can't get married to boys.' Later on, putting her to bed, I brought up the fact that I know girls who are married to girls (a bit of a lie; they're not legally married) and I know boys who are married to boys. She said, 'No, no,' because she never sees that anywhere, right? So I had to give her examples of some lesbians she knows. Then she's like, 'Oh, okay.' "

To achieve something better for her family than a minimum-wage existence, Dana enrolled in college following Sylvia's birth. There, her nascent feminism was thrown for a loop when she found herself having to empathize with students who encountered the world very differently. "You know how women's studies is women, women, women, meaning every woman experiences the same thing?" she muses. "Well, when I began taking women's studies, I didn't quite understand the invisibility that women of colour faced." Unconsciously, she acted like the people who had earlier brushed off her struggles with motherhood: she did not listen. "For a long time, I so much wanted everything to be okay that I was more worried about how I sounded than whether I was racist. I didn't want to appear racist because I didn't want to be challenged."

Then something "clicked" in one of her classes. A serious discussion about building bridges among marginalized communities got bogged down in—you guessed it—the hierarchy of oppression. "There was a big emotional upset where a woman of colour told a white woman, 'What you just said was very racist.' The white woman shot back, 'If I can't say it in a women's studies class, where can I say it? Now I'm being silenced. Now I'm this, now I'm that.' " Right there, it dawned on Dana that micro-marginalizing each other is a dead end. Sorry, she shrugs, but equating a challenge to being silenced "is not a satisfactory answer to the charge that you're racist. It's only skirting the issue and shutting down debate." Yet, I wonder, do we not need to feel some comfort to engage each other? "Everybody needs comfort zones," she answers, "but if we get too comfortable that means somebody has the world all figured out and we're just absorbing it instead of creating it." After that incident, Dana says, "it just didn't matter any more how I appeared; it mattered whether I was racist."

She attended another class in which a woman who raised the issue of racism did not return, prompting Dana to look at why she, herself, came back. She concluded that her mother's self-educated outlook, plus her grandmother's work as a teacher, fostered an affinity with the classroom that others, including those from economically privileged backgrounds, could not claim. Moreover, being white, Dana saw herself reflected in the classroom authorities—the professors. Despite minor discomforts, she did not have to bend much to belong there. That is some power. Ruminating on various filters of identity and their links to empowerment, Dana discovered that she could have more agency than she once assumed.

Given that cache of agency, "I had to get past the drive to shelter myself and my emotions." As soon as she did, Dana started to listen. "I let go of my assumptions, especially this 'Come on, I'm not racist' bit, because if I can expect others to reevaluate their sexism, why shouldn't I be expected to reevaluate my racism? I had to sit back and go, 'Okay, people are telling me something out of my realm of experience and I've got to take note. Then I need to learn what that has to do with me.' "

That Dana disciplined her impulses to pull herself up from the cycle of defensiveness should make any neo-conservative proud. Exercising such personal control is no minor achievement, considering how many of us have been programmed to cry "political correctness" when dared to reconsider our words or deeds. Dana sees through that version of victimhood. "No way do I have it all worked out," she stresses, "but if I say something racist I'm now open to someone challenging me and I won't fall apart. It means that I can change." Risking one step towards the bigger picture of justice can inject a new momentum into personal agency—and social solidarity.

Her own working-class status puts Dana in a similarly challenging relationship to fellow feminists, from whom she sometimes feels the pressure to purchase conscience. "I can't afford the $10 or $14 children's books from feminist stores," Dana says matter of factly. "I can't go to the co-op and spend $20 on Bridgehead coffee. It really bugs me that I have to go to the superstore and buy no-name brands when they get their goods from the lowest-paid workers and the least ethical companies. But it's something that I have to swallow."

The most rousing rhetoric about resisting corporate culture cannot hide the paradox that Dana has just described: consumer feminism is the path of least resistance for many women, the most convenient way to flash their soldiers' stripes. For Dana, however, fighting back takes more effort. And more imagination. So entrenched is consumer feminism that it starts at the specialty coffee shop and leads straight to the steps of the local advocacy centre. "I'd love to volunteer at the Vancouver Status of Women office, but I can't even afford the $4.50 bus fare to get there and back. I'm more worried about getting to the Ministry of Social Services and pleading my case for a medical receipt."

Still, the irksome ironies of being a working-class feminist might have the makings of true transformation. Dana hopes that all the crazy contradictions mean "I'm less judgemental; I understand that people do what they need to do to survive." She pauses again. Her statement of empathy—all of us do what we can—strangely teases out more agency—can I do better? "I know women who are totally dedicated to their children, their careers and their political activities, and I have to say that I'm not one of those super-jugglers. But I'm always pushing myself to explore how much I can do considering my circumstances." A few more moments of contemplation pass. "Of course, I'm racked by questions. Doing the house-y thing, fitting into what others would look at as pretty typical heterosexual behaviour—is it in conflict with the changes that have to happen in this world and in our homes? Or am I doing the reasonable thing, back-pedalling from time to time to try to make my situation work?" Asking these questions feels like a sell-out, Dana admits, "but it's really a balancing act."

For all of her martial arts moxie, Claire Huang Kinsley poses plenty of questions to herself. "You can have this incredible tool kit of skills to deal with any situation," says the twenty-eight-year-old self-defence instructor, "but that doesn't mean you have all the answers."

Then again, some of her answers seem to work. Late one night, after my first self-defence class with Claire, I walked to a convenience store in my Toronto neighbourhood. Peering at me through his window, a driver slowed down as he cruised past. He parked in front of the store just as I entered it. When I came out, I saw him sitting in his rusty Oldsmobile, several feet away, motor running. He stared at me; I returned the favour. To let him know I was aware, I bellowed his licence plate number twice—a tactic taught by Claire only hours before. Then I headed back to my place using an alternate route, another of Claire's suggestions. When I spun around, the man was gone.

Maybe the guy had no intent to harm me. Maybe he was craning out the window to search for a street name rather than to track my steps. Maybe he stopped at the store to check a map and happened to look up at the very moment I caught his glance.

But maybe not.

Regardless, a potentially dangerous situation had been averted. (Drunk on the resulting confidence surge, I toyed with the idea of selling her future graduates T-shirts that scream "Trained by Claire, so beware!" Tacky but true, gleefully capitalist but hawked with a conscience.) When I told Claire about my corner-store confrontation, she congratulated me and, characteristically, took little credit. "Self-defence is about drawing from your own power," she said. "I can't do that for you; I can only help you get ready."

The program she teaches is Wen-Do, a patchwork English-Japanese term which roughly means "women's way." Claire read about it in a Montreal newspaper and signed up the year it was offered at her school. Once there, she says, "I was hooked." Wen-Do's lessons include basic physical manoeuvres: releasing choke holds, kicking targets and blocking hits. What distinguishes the program—and hooked Claire—is its feminist edge. Wen-Do stresses the social and cultural contexts of violence so that women emerge emotionally equipped as well as physically prepared. "It got me to start thinking about why violence happens," Claire testifies, "and it was the first experience that led me to define myself as a feminist."

The Toronto couple who founded Wen-Do considered feminism to be a necessary feature. In 1972, they launched the program as a response to the murder of a woman that took place immediately outside her New York City apartment building. Many witnessed the attack, hearing her cries for help but doing nothing. "The founders of Wen-Do realized that what women have always been told—'depend on other people to protect you'—wasn't realistic," Claire says. With or without an empathetic society, "self-reliance is the first and last line of defence."

To be sure, it was empathy—rather than a personal crisis—that guided her decision to try Wen-Do at age sixteen. "Although I had a very happy childhood, free of abuse and intimidation, I didn't have to be personally hit or grabbed or pushed around to be profoundly affected by violence," she explains. "So many of my friends have been attacked or threatened that the rage I feel when someone close tells me about it is impossible to describe. I decided that even if I'm going to be outraged about violence, I'm not going to be helpless."

In 1990, Claire moved to Toronto and found a job in community services. But, itching to "be pro-active," she looked up Wen-Do in the phone book. Upon finding the listing, "I knew I had aspirations to become an instructor, even though I'd only finished the first fifteen hours of the course."

In more ways than one, taking Wen-Do introduced Claire to the possibilities of flexing agency. She went in thinking that violence against women is like a natural disaster—it cannot be prevented; it can only be coped with. She came out with a new understanding of the range of choices, and the reservoir of authority, within her reach. "At one point in my life, quiet was all I knew how to be. Now I feel I have more strings to my bow. I can be loud and commanding when necessary." My burning ears back that up. I have heard Claire yell "Huuuuh!" like nobody's business. "Thankfully," she adds, "I've never had to hit anyone."

Instead, Claire uses Wen-Do to stay aware of her surroundings and to draw boundaries. Although she no longer apologizes for having boundaries, establishing them continues to test her confidence. "Just a few days ago, the superintendent asked if he could come up and fix the windows in my apartment. I said, 'I have to go out at 3:00 p.m.; could you do it before then?' He said, 'Well, I have a key to your place and I could do it after as well.' And I said, 'This has nothing to do with you personally, but I prefer not to have people in my apartment when I'm not there.' For me, this took a conscious effort. I felt it was important for my own sense of privacy. But at the same time, there were all of these voices whispering: Is he going to think that I don't trust him? That I'm afraid he's going to steal my stuff?" So how did the super respond? I ask. "He just said, 'Okey doke, fine.' It wasn't a big deal to him, but to have raised the issue at all was a big deal for me. So, to this day, being clear about my limits is a process of negotiation. It's not a given."

As with just about everyone profiled in this chapter, negotiation is for Claire a deliberate strategy that fosters enough temporary comfort to allow for further action. But, she adds, it is a comfort that she has to feel with herself as much as with anyone else. Some of her students find it difficult to yell "because they don't want to take up *too* much space. When you think about the images we have of loud women, it's like they're hysterical, crazy, ranting. They're taking up more space than they should be *permitted*. That's the context in which a lot of women have learned not to be assertive, but assertiveness doesn't have to mean that you don't listen. What it means is that you're comfortable negotiating your space. You can only do that when you have choices and accept your authority to make them."

Violence is the absence of negotiation; agency without empathy. Which is why, despite her wonderful childhood, Claire felt so strongly about teaching self-defence: "I wanted to give choices back." Hence her sense of accountability. Considering the central role that choices play in Claire's life, not only as a self-defence teacher but also as a mixed-race woman, she is compelled to take responsibility for how those choices are exercised. "Part of self-defence is knowing you'll make less-than-ideal choices from time to time," she acknowledges, referring not so much to tackling thugs as to handling mundane, morally fluid offences.

In one story that contrasts with Dana Putnam's, Claire dealt with a vastly different but equally troublesome side of racism. "I was standing in line with a bunch of people waiting for a theatre workshop to begin, and this young white woman cracked a racist remark about Chinese people. Because I've got light skin, I don't think she knew I was part Asian. So part of me was saying, 'Of course I should challenge her.' Then part of me was saying, 'Why should I have to do the educating?' Another part of me was saying, 'But she doesn't realize that I'm Asian, so if I don't say anything, it looks like a 'white' person—me—excusing another white person.' Not only would I be complicit in her racism; I would be 'passing' for a white person."

Ultimately, Claire chose not to say anything. "Looking back on it, I don't have a clear idea of what I would have said to her. I could have said, 'That's racist.' I could have said, 'My mother's Chinese' and just let her put the pieces together. I could have said, 'I'm of Chinese descent and I find your comments really hurtful.' But I still can't pick the best response. There is no best."

What Claire does know is not to berate herself about failing to confront people because "the world being what it is, I'm going to have lots more chances to practice." Often being mistaken for a white person guarantees this. " 'Passing' protects me from the more blatant expressions of racism that others get, but, in an ironic way, it also means that sometimes I'm there when people say things that they have the rudimentary courtesy—or hypocrisy—not to say around other people."

Thus, she builds self-defence savvy by learning from her mistakes. After that incident in the line-up, Claire faced another situation at work. "A client and I were in the middle of something totally routine and all of a sudden he started complaining that there were too many Chinese and Vietnamese immigrants coming to this country. I just said, 'My mother's Chinese' and watched him squirm. He looked abashed. He was like, 'Oh ... well, you don't look very Chinese.' I was like, 'That doesn't help at all.' " I almost anticipate a "Huuuuh!" to let off some steam. Instead, she lets out a laugh. "Because I let myself take a different tack with the older guy [than with the young woman in the line-up], I felt a genuine sense of power."

Claire keeps herself honest by focussing on the power she wields. Dana Putnam strives for similar accountability. "I've chosen my feminism and my family," she declares, "and I'm committed to both of them. That

means I'm responsible for controlling how I use the power I've got."
Dana also believes that "if I can learn this for myself, then maybe feminism can learn it too. As long as feminists keep changing from within,
there will be a spot for every person. Every person and each of their
experiences."

But let us be frank: accountability is the summit of sincerity. For that reason, it is seldom reached. We can all fake empathy. We can take half-
hearted stabs at agency. But accountability is the final measure of
commitment to others, bringing us face to face with the question: Do we
really want to change our conduct for the benefit of more people than
just ourselves? Fabrication will eventually be found out. Thomas
Ponniah does not buy the phrase "police accountability," while Trudy Parsons lambastes the lack of media accountability.

Sadia Zaman does too. As a journalist, she is not only publicizing the
dearth of responsibility in her craft; she is helping to replenish it. Can the
results of empathy and agency always be sealed by asserting the value of
accountability?

CHAPTER 7

accountability

Usually, Sadia Zaman is soft-spoken, even self-effacing. But not on one November day in 1992, when she made her presence felt at a meeting of some powerful Canadian journalists in Ottawa. "I often feel walking into a room like this the way many of you must have felt walking into boardrooms full of men. I don't see myself here," said the TV producer, now thirty-one, to the hushed crowd.

The annual Women in the Media conference involves many big names and valuable contacts. With past keynote speakers such as women's rights activist Robin Morgan and singing legend Buffy Sainte-Marie, the gathering is a feminist refuelling station for many newswomen. A proud feminist, the South Asian Sadia differed. She noted that all the talk at this seminar on the portrayal of women swooped in on sexism. But, she asked, does racism play no part in female stereotypes? Her impromptu remarks, erupting from somewhere in the back half of the audience, stopped the panelists in their progressive political tracks. Finally, panel member Michele Landsberg, the *Toronto Star*'s plucky feminist columnist, blurted, "Who are you?" Suspending her usual humility, Sadia stepped forward. Landsberg accepted her point graciously.

Three years later, Sadia was among the principal organizers of the Women in the Media conference. Held in polyglot Toronto, the event attracted more journalists of colour than ever. Sadia saw to it that invitations got to them, not out of a personal desire to dictate but out of a professional need to share power. "It took time to reach the people who are usually overlooked," she affirms. Still, as when she helps other journalists find women of colour to interview, or when she hears of a job opportunity and sifts through her file of resumés for underemployed women of colour to call, Sadia believes that "responsibility comes with having access."

Being a broadcaster—literally, someone who transmits messages to the masses—she also enjoys the power to help mould public perceptions. Her filter consists of three convictions. One: "If I, as a journalist, don't care about the people I cover, then distortion is inevitable." Two: "Anything that doesn't accurately reflect who we are is, by definition, a lie. A lot of TV is a lie for that reason." Three: "I'm concerned with making sure TV's a little bit closer to telling the truth." Not deluded about how much of the TV lie she alone can correct, neither does Sadia downplay her opportunities. "I've got a hell of a lot of clout in terms of which images are shot, how scripts are written, how tapes are edited," she observes. She accepts that from her "little perch," she cannot undo the genocidal horrors of Bosnia and Rwanda, but she can report on the activities of former Yugoslavians and of expatriate Rwandans in Canada. "For problems that seem so overwhelming and muddled, I've found some very, very small but manageable solutions," Sadia says, "and they come from doing things that I care about." Such as leaving the mainstream media for Vision TV.

Sadia landed her first reporting gig at the *Wynyard Advance*, a weekly newspaper in her home province of Saskatchewan. After a summer of dashing from fires to fairs, from the town hall to the annual chicken chariot race (where it is unclear who clucks more—the cheering spectators or the chickens pulling paper chariots), she realized that she "really loved this journalism thing." Over the next few years, during which she wrote about refugee camps on the Thai-Cambodian border and reported for a Regina TV station, Sadia also developed "a deep love" for the worldliness of the CBC. In 1987, the girl from Lanigan, Saskatchewan, moved to the CBC newsroom in Sydney, Nova Scotia, ending up, in 1990, at the national radio newsroom as a writer and editor.

"It was an exciting time in journalism," Sadia remembers. She points to the armed stand-off near Oka, Quebec, a seventy-eight-day confrontation between the Mohawk village of Kanesatake and all manner of government agents, sparked after the municipality of Oka unilaterally decided to extend its golf course into a pine forest claimed by Mohawk people for three hundred years. A native blockade, a provincial police raid and an eighty-six-bullet shoot-out left one corporal dead. The restless Canadian summer had just begun. Then, sure as Schwartzkopf, came a winter of war. Iraq's invasion of Kuwait escalated into U.S. missiles careening over the Persian Gulf, accompanied by the most massive propaganda campaign since Vietnam. If the theatre of combat appeared thousands of miles from Canada, the distrust engendered by it hit home in the sudden harassment of Arab-Canadians by federal security officials.

As a result of those clashes, Sadia discovered her profound dissatisfaction with the narrow scope of opinion in mainstream journalism. "For the first time, I questioned the stereotypes and assumptions prevalent in the media. I believed the problems were systemic, so I began to question my own role within the system." In 1991, Toronto-based Vision TV offered her the job of creating social justice documentaries for the human affairs program *It's About Time*. With scarce hesitation, Sadia vacated the CBC for a place where "I could challenge old images about my fellow Canadians."

Wealthier networks have since attempted to lure her from Vision, but she chooses to stay because "there is no disparity between what I know to be the complicated truth about people's lives and what goes on that screen." Paradoxically, remaining at Vision has less to do with being stationary than with being progressive. To maintain integrity and advance curiosity, then, distortion is something for which Sadia feels she must hold herself and other members of the media accountable.

Her own accountability starts with taking advantage of the "incredible support" she receives at Vision TV. The world's only channel licenced to explore the innumerable facets of faith, Vision understands that value-free journalism is a crock, and thus the national network makes no bones about its primary value: that individuals, by virtue of being individuals, come in all packages. Amid so much casual complacency in the media, Vision's speciality—point-of-view journalism—stands out as advocacy. (To be sure, advocacy can have its injustices: the nine-year-old network is widely, often rightly, criticized as a pulpit for shameless televangelists such as gay-baiting Jerry Falwell and Republican commissar Pat Robertson. By the same token, in 1996 Vision stopped airing the sermons of a Sikh separatist who routinely lauded violence against the government of India. The station warned *Ankhila Punjab*'s incendiary host at least three times; his diatribes, however, continued. After Vision slapped a six-month suspension on the show, a cluster of Sikh fundamentalists descended upon network headquarters in protest. The decision stood—for a few weeks, anyway. Talk soon followed to reinstate *Ankhila Punjab* early, albeit under stricter adherence to Canadian broadcast laws.)

Whatever the politics behind its explicitly religious programming, Vision's journalism is in a different stream—different enough to have me working in it since 1994. And different enough to have attracted the acclaim of Canada's TV industry in 1993. *It's About Time*, then coproduced and hosted by Sadia, earned a prestigious Gemini Award for best reflecting the country's cultural diversity. Episodes have featured a Jewish family in the Northwest Territories, American draft dodgers who have settled in Canada and a critical analysis of Sunday mornings at churches, this being "the most segregated time" of the Canadian week.

Although the pace of progressive journalism can be gruelling—laziness does not unpack stereotypes; it only preserves them—Sadia says, "I'm never exhausted because I don't have to fight the politics and the material is always interesting." In one of her most exhilarating professional moments, she travelled to South Africa to profile a white Jewish woman and a brown Muslim woman. Both felt an ethical duty to work with black people and begin reversing the wrongs of apartheid. Among the myths undermined by Sadia's South African profiles are those of insular warfare between Jews and Muslims, of immediate liberation for people of colour in the post-apartheid era and of African women as downtrodden creatures. "The fact is, throughout the world you're going to find individuals challenging their societies," Sadia tells me. "My contribution is highlighting some of that in a way which says, 'So what if this woman's wearing a scarf on her head? Let's concentrate on the fact that she's dodging bullets in a squadron camp.' " On that trip to South Africa, Sadia deliberately assembled a multiracial production crew made up of local talent. "They knew the realities of the country better than I did," she shrugs. "My pieces were improved, made more truthful, by their sensitivities." The crew included only one woman, a sound technician, but she nonetheless paved the way for the permanent audio woman at Vision TV today.

Sadia's toughness, which she clarifies as a "refusal to compromise essential values like anti-racism," can also be seen in her off-screen life. Her marriage to a white-skinned Prairie boy, business consultant Neil Iddon, "was a choice that I knew would involve fighting other people's generalizations about white men." The story of how they met attests to Sadia's driving belief in telling the truth. After running into a car in the parking lot of a Regina pizza place, she rushed inside the restaurant to find the car's owner. He was having lunch with Neil. In September 1992—several years since the wreck—Neil and Sadia married. The moral: "Be honest when you hit a stranger's car," Sadia half-seriously proposes. "Your life may change for the better because of it."

Although initially ambivalent about marrying Neil—since childhood, says Sadia, "I thought marriage would mean giving up too much of myself"—his values convinced her she could be her true self while maturing as a person and as a professional. "When I get nervous about things," Sadia explains, "Neil takes it for granted that I can accomplish my goal, whatever it happens to be. That's such a strong message. I absorb it. I get courage from it." For instance, she was preparing a documentary for the fifth anniversary of the Montreal Massacre. "I spent hours interviewing the mother of one of the women who'd been killed. Everything she said about her daughter's life, and how she managed to turn a tragedy into helping other women—it meant the world to me. When I got home, I couldn't hold in my emotions any more. When Neil got home, I was on the couch crying. He didn't say anything. He knew I'd been in Montreal filming this thing, and he just understood." Neil makes it easier for Sadia to integrate responsibility at home and the office because, like the journalistic ethic at Vision TV, he does not work against her. Better still, he works with her. "Neil can't stand it when people are treated unfairly," Sadia notes, "and to him, 'people' automatically include women."

But the relationship has not been all sweetness and light. Sadia expected to be culturally audited by many South Asians for choosing a white man as her husband. Her expectations were fulfilled. "We went into a shop where the owner saw the two of us together," begins Sadia's tale of going to Toronto's "Little India" district in search of the perfect wedding dress. "He had all the dresses hanging on the wall. I said, 'How much is that particular one?' He said, 'I don't sell wedding dresses here.' I said, 'Well, what's that?' All he said was, 'I don't sell wedding dresses here' and walked away. It reminded me that choices come with consequences and that each of us has some responsibility in that."

What, though, does responsibility mean for a mixed marriage? That the couple keep a low profile in the likes of Little India? That they advise the shop owner to join the 1990s? That they sue him for denying service to customers based on their skin combinations? All are options, but Sadia prefers a longer-term responsibility. "Ultimately, it means that when we have kids we'll have to make sure to give them a strong basis of identity," namely, "self-worth, and children get that by knowing there's a place for them."

Last June, Sadia and Neil had a daughter, Samarah Zaman Iddon. Census data on biracial Canadians is not readily available, but according to a recent ABC newscast, the number of mixed-race Americans under the age of eighteen has quadrupled in the last quarter century to two million. Whether or not the same trend can be extrapolated to Canada, Sadia and Neil do worry about their daughter "passing" for white and thus not being aware of her heritages. They also worry about Samarah being subjected, like Claire Huang Kinsley, to back-door racism. As such, months before Samarah's arrival, Neil and Sadia moved downtown so that the baby could grow up in a neighbourhood and school with a motley, polyphonous gaggle of children. They also intend to give Samarah "a good sense of who her grandparents are—on both sides—starting with a homemade book on our family histories."

People with a sense of obligation to younger generations are the new mother's personal role models. Dr. Rita Shelton Deverell, a cofounder of Vision TV, ranks as one of Sadia's mentors and is an animating spirit behind Sadia's belief in mutual responsibility. "It goes full circle: when I mentor other young women of colour, Rita's the one I look to for guidance," Sadia says. "Again, here's somebody who just lives her life and doesn't sit around whining about her circumstances as a black woman."

Whining, hardly. But fighting marginalization, most assuredly. A veteran actor raised in the segregated southern U.S., Deverell has on more than one occasion battled the CBC's unwillingness to let her audition for certain roles, including that of a farm woman, because she is black. In her multi-stage career, Deverell has portrayed pioneer feminist Nellie McClung, Prime Minister John A. Macdonald and a plethora of Shakespearean characters, thanks to her persistence and the sharing of parental duties by her husband, playwright Rex Deverell. Sadia met her future mentor at the University of Regina's respected School of Journalism and Communications, where Deverell was teaching. After working her way up to direct the school, Deverell hopped channels to help inaugurate Vision TV. Popularly called "the face of Vision" or, as I have heard many viewers put it, "that crazy lady with the flower in her hair," Deverell is currently the network's vice-president of production and presentation. In that capacity, she regularly appears on-camera with Vision's vice-president of programming to read, then respond to, viewer mail. As she explains, "We want people to know that their letters haven't vanished into some bureaucratic ether."

Deverell's fusion of audacity and accountability has shown Sadia the possibilities of participation. "I used to think that bitterness towards men was a prerequisite for joining the feminist movement, but Rita's reinforced the fact that I don't have to do things the way everybody else does them. I mean, I never felt angry at men. I lived in a house with three brothers and a father, and I'm married to a guy who 'gets it,' you know? Women share a lot with men and I think that's especially true of women of colour. Men [of colour] get out there and they're discriminated against, too, so if you force me to choose my alliances strictly along gender lines, then my choice is clear: I'll take whatever lets me be a whole person."

Integrity is the main reason that Sadia takes her chances sounding off at media colleagues. "This isn't a popular thing to say but I'll tell you anyway," she prepares me. "I can deal with sexism in the newsroom. It's the racism that tears me apart. When I went to that [Women in the Media] conference and I saw women who I know are not the most supportive when it comes to fighting racism and I heard them talk about inequality, it alienated me. Everything was sexism, sexism, sexism, and if you face racism, go discuss it in that corner." She says that until white women consider racism as much their issue as hers—until they bring an empathy to it—then no woman in any workplace will be accepted for her full self, be it as a journalist or as a feminist. Out of mutual interest and responsibility, "this connection has to be made."

Was it made at that conference? Sadia's hope wrestles with her hesitation. "To hear somebody with Michele Landsberg's power and profile finally express that yeah, racism is a serious issue—I'd like to believe it made the difference to the other women there. But I'm not sure because I remember, above everything else, silence. The room got very, very quiet. People just didn't know how to take it, I think.

"Someday, when I'm up there and a nervous young woman says something to me in a room full of strangers, I'll remember the silence, remember it strongly."

With this final statement, as with her statement that caring about the people she covers prevents journalistic distortion, Sadia testifies to the link between empathy and accountability. Agency bridges them, rendering this definition: Accountability is the willingness to be held responsible for what we choose to do and not do. It stops us from soaring into the stratosphere at the expense of those to whom we feel a connection.

The connotation is that accountability limits each individual's potential to achieve. In some ways, yes. But in more ways, no. Accountability does not restrict our capacity to achieve so much as our capacity to deceive, to get away with saying one thing and doing another. Moreover, if people were led by the values of empathy and agency, then our accountability to each other could actually free our individual talents by allowing us to express who we genuinely are. As Sadia notes, her partnership with Neil—their mutual accountability—gives her the confidence "to accomplish [her] goals, whatever they happen to be." Above all, when my accountability is anchored in empathy, then I am not responsible only to others; I am also responsible to myself. That means I have a stake in seeing things through, thereby pushing my potential to imagine, create and get the job properly done. As such, accountability is not just a decision; it is a process.

Then again, Nellie McClung got the job done, and her most famous statement appears to reject accountability. The early twentieth-century suffragist, whose determination helped make Manitoba women the first in Canada to win the vote, urged fellow social activists to "Never retreat, never explain, never apologize. Get the thing done and let them howl." But this was her exasperated reply to the repeated unaccountability of power-holders. The value that McClung placed on accountability shines through in the first of her major political speeches, when she declared that dignity should be accorded to the "left-out people" because "everybody can tell us something or give us a new point of view."

In 1911, a group of women lobbied the Law Amendments Committee of the Manitoba parliament to protect widows against husbands who would deny them a rightful share of property. The attorney-general assured his petitioners that "a husband is never far wrong, and is better capable than anyone else of judging what he should leave his wife. If he leaves her penniless, there is good reason."

Shortly thereafter, McClung and another activist approached Manitoba Premier Sir Rodmond Roblin to appoint a female social worker as inspector of Winnipeg's sweatshops. They even took the reluctant Roblin on a tour of these women-filled wastelands. But the filth he saw and the fumes he ingested merely convinced the premier that regulating such places "is no job for a woman. I have too much respect for women to give them any job like this." Once more, the government would not listen. This pattern of intentional deafness persuaded a few radicals to launch the nonpartisan Political Equality League and a campaign for the female franchise. Having acquired 10,000 signatures on petitions, the little lady leaguers went back to the Manitoba legislature in January 1914. Proclaimed McClung to Roblin, "We are not here to ask for a reform, or a gift, or a favour ... but for justice." Her appeal culminated in an emphasis on the value of accountability. "[W]e have come to the last ditch in our onward march towards freedom ... and we are stretching our hands to you to help us over. Sir Rodmond, it is your move." The pompous premier was moved only to rise from his seat and launch into a lecture about why women should not hold their collective breath. Write McClung biographers Mary Hallett and Marilyn Davis, "[Roblin] assured that if their cause was just, they would eventually succeed, though he neglected to say in which century." Accustomed to being rebuffed, McClung took careful note of Sir Rodmond's words and mannerisms during his lecture, observations that would add authenticity to the mock parliament that the PEL organized for the next evening.

By posing as female legislators in a make-believe land that refused men the vote, the suffragists sought to build empathy—if not among male parliamentarians then at least among male citizens. Before a full house, the dramatization unfolded. Two petitions were presented, one wanting a ban on certain articles of men's clothing and the other asking for work-saving devices for men. While some opposition members looked lost in their needlepoint, others heckled the petitioners with such lines as, "You just want to get on right with men!" Then arrived the male contingent with a wheelbarrow of petitions demanding the vote. Premier McClung listened intently but disagreed with a mixture of sporadic scorn, annoyance, tolerance, courtesy and piety. "The modesty of our men, which we reverence, forbids us giving them the vote. Man's place is on the farm," she said, wrapping up. "Perhaps the time may come when men may vote with women—but in the meantime be of good cheer." Unlike the audience, whose roars of delight brought new supporters and money to the campaign, Sir Rodmond was not of good cheer after that performance.

Given the Conservative government's continued intransigence, and the Liberal Party's willingess to join the PEL's crusade, the suffragists had no choice but to go partisan. McClung followed Roblin incessantly during the 1914 Manitoba election, which the Conservatives won but with a much smaller majority and a plunging popular vote. Not long after, Conservative scandals necessitated another election—this time sweeping the Liberals into power. They granted the vote to Manitoba women on January 28, 1916, a full two years after suffragists offered Conservatives the olive branch of reason and received patronizing pats in return. It is because the powers that be felt no compunction to hear the "left-out people" that McClung resolved to "get the job done and let them howl." The lesson is, for one party to be accountable, all parties must be accountable, once again suggesting that we cannot cut ourselves off from each other without serious consequences.

It appears, though, that some need further prodding to heed that lesson. Indeed, some need to face contemporary suffragists such as the Women's Constituency Group (WCG), a handful of students—including a man—who pressed their university to share responsibility for preventing assaults on campus. Between September 1992 and 1993, the WCG unearthed what its members call a cover-up of rapes at the University of Prince Edward Island. With a mixture of rudeness and shrewdness, they convinced a recalcitrant administration to open a women's centre that would serve the safety of all students.

Hardly easy going, especially against the backdrop of flesh-eating campus politics. In fall 1991, for example, the "Woman's Page" of the *X-Press*, UPEI's student newspaper, printed an article on how to guard against date rape. Its basic message was that this *could* happen to you. Two male sociology students responded by whipping off a weekly column called "The Backlash," which generated a war of words and a rapid-fire exchange of personal attacks in letters to the editor. The WCG could not count on a sympathetic press.

Taking on the establishment proved even more daunting for those like Lori Duckworth, now twenty-six, who had no experience with justice movements. Still, she had a strong sense of personal agency. "In our generation, you grow up thinking you can conquer the world," Lori shrugs, her island lilt and baby face contrasting sharply with the resolute puffs she takes of her cigarette. "When I was a little girl, there was never the assumption that you can't do what you wanted because you're a woman or a girl. I never heard that. Plus, I've always been really involved in the United Church. Growing up, I thought the church was woman-friendly because, hey, I had two female ministers.

"So how could there be an elite, or even a structure, that pretended it didn't have to change?" she asks, referring to the university administration. "That was my mentality for the longest time." But in the span of one week, Lori lost nine pounds and many of her old beliefs. She also helped found the WCG.

It all started when the local CBC TV broke the story—some say the tale—that a first-year female student at UPEI had bolted out of a "get-acquainted" dorm party and wound up in hospital for assault-related injuries. (Weeks later, UPEI public relations officer Gerry Birt disclosed that Charlottetown City Police found "no medical or physical evidence to indicate the victim was beaten." At the time, however, doctors did not see fit to release the student for several days.) Although UPEI began an investigation immediately after the alleged assault, the CBC newscast suggested that university security lacked public confidence. After all, it was someone close to the survivor's family who handed the CBC this story, having received no commitment from the university that justice would ensue. By now, the reported rape was almost a week old, UPEI had not made a substantive comment about it, and the university president, William Eliot, left town that afternoon.

Disturbed by the news and revved up after her women's studies class that night, Lori resolved to raise a political stink for the first time in her life. She drafted a petition demanding the university first deplore sexual violence, then take measures to stop more of it from happening on campus. "My mom typed up the petition for me because my hands were shaking," Lori recalls. "I was nervous and naive—very naive. I didn't know the first thing about activism."

The next day she brought copies of the petition to school and, with the help of a few friends, started to circulate them. Hundreds of students spread the word; soon, they had accumulated 1,500 signatures. The heat was on. In the afternoon, the administration prepared a brief media statement acknowledging that the alleged victim had laid a formal complaint with UPEI security.

That evening, Lori discovered that the issue of rape hit closer to home than she had imagined. Moved by her petition, a member of Lori's family revealed that she was once gang-raped and, as a result, had undergone twenty-five years of psychiatric assessment. "It was a shock," Lori says. "By the time I got to the university the next morning, I was still scared, but now that I knew someone who'd been raped, there was no way I could be scared *off*." For what lay in store, she would need the fortification.

Within a day, TV and print reporters caught wind of the petition and flocked to UPEI for the next round of coverage. The administration gave sketchy interviews, frustrating what many students called their "need to know." Bad weather only encouraged students to move a near-spontaneous rally inside the campus amphitheatre, where they competed with media for every square inch of space. Winston Pineau, the dean of science, accepted Lori's petition on behalf of the still-absent President Eliot.

Under a national spotlight, the university finally responded—sort of. "We got our butts hauled into security to be interrogated," Lori says of herself and a friend. There, she continues, security officers unexpectedly divulged that they knew of another male student who had assaulted at least five women and that, as they put it, " 'it's all taken care of.' " Lori's decoding of the statement: *that* rapist had been transferred to a different school.

The budding activists left stunned. "I didn't realize the implications of what they'd told us," Lori admits. Nor, she hints, did she want to fathom the implications. "I'd spent three years and a lot of money at UPEI, and I didn't know if they were going to suspend me, put me on probation, or what. So when I got out of there unscathed, it was relief, not outrage, that set in."

By week's end, the media scrutiny had grown intense enough for President Eliot to return home and hold a public "information forum." Some nine hundred people attended, almost half of them men. Beyond those details, Lori's rendition of the forum diverges from the administration's. Sticking to a recital of "the facts," PR man Gerry Birt presented President Eliot as having "apologize[d] for the handling of the situation ... He says he will address campus safety in all its aspects and promises that if changes are not made he will step down. He pledges to take action to address concerns about the issue of sexual violence against women." But Lori has a less rosy recollection of the president's accountability. At one point, she says, a student asked how many rapes on campus the security officials knew about. With Dr. Eliot and the student council president standing beside him, the security chief claimed there were "no records" of

other rapes. To Lori, it was a semantic twirl within a free-skating deception. "I could have easily stood up and said, 'Wait a minute, I was just interrogated by your officers and they told me of these incidents. Five of them.'
But I was too scared."

Nonetheless, she and a few others realized the potential for secrecy
surrounding campus assault—and formed the Women's Constituency
Group, named in a rush, to fight this deficit of accountability. "We knew
that if we let the issue go, that would've been the end of it right there,"
says Christeena Murphy, a group member.

In that sense, the WCG was a way to address not only the university's
inactivity but also the students' own tendency to sweep sexual violence
aside in the scramble to get on with life. "I only lived in residence for about
four months, but during that time I heard of a number of date rapes," says
Shelley Carroll, another early WCG member. "Sad thing was, we heard
about it today and forgot about it tomorrow. Nothing was ever done."
Although "tired of the bubble," she sensed no peer support until the WCG
came along. "Finally, I found some people that I could talk to about these
things. Now we could talk to each other, we could talk to President Eliot,
we could even talk to the media. We could start making things happen."

And they did, under often vicious circumstances. Their first challenge
enmired them in the snarky, murky morass of the political correctness battles raging across Canadian campuses. Within a week of the WCG's inauguration, some UPEI sociology majors, deeming themselves "Students for
Free Speech and Academic Rights," announced that they would be screening a film called *Cannibal Women in the Avocado Jungle of Death*. They had
picked a fraternity-favoured T-and-A flick, starring former *Playboy* bunny
Shannon Tweed, as a slap to the feminist purity-wardens who supposedly
run the country's universities. In one scene that depicts a close encounter
with gang rape, the Tweed character emerges from her primitive cham-
bers, peels several men off of a woman, then sternly asks the woman why
she would be out there in her nightgown. "Kind of putting the blame on
her," Lori observes, "which is exactly what a lot of people were doing on
campus [to the alleged rape victim]. You know, 'What was that girl doing
in a male dormitory?' "

Still, the WCG did not seek to ban the film from university premises,
only to delay its screening until the wounds of recent weeks had passed.
"Our argument was, show *Cannibal Women* if you want but pick a better

time at least. We've just been dealing with a reported rape," Christeena explains.

So the WCG asked university administrators to intervene. For Heather Morrison, one of the group's most committed members, the stress of waiting for an answer proved particularly acute: her aunt was a counsellor at UPEI but would not acknowledge violence against women to be a problem on campus. "I was totally on edge," Heather remembers of the night university officials convened to discuss the fate of *Cannibal Women*. As if she had swallowed pins and needles, Heather even threw up in the bathroom of a women's studies professor. Finally, the decision: an administration emissary would speak with the free-speechers about postponing their campus screening of *Cannibal Women*. (They complied for a few days.) The WCG had scored its first, fragile victory.

With it came a savaging in the student press. The WCG endured editorial accusations of "high-handedness," "hypocrisy" (for not having protested sexual thriller *Basic Instinct*) and the predictable comparisons to book-burning. One student sardonically recommended that the WCG raid a local library for its "rare selection of 'pornography' written by 'dead old white guys.'" All such criticisms missed the WCG's point about sensitive timing. Small wonder. Much of the criticism owed its ferocity to the grander campus duels over zero-tolerance policies, in which even cultural kitsch can assume constitutional weight. Once tacky artifacts like *Cannibal Women* take on mythic proportions, the timing becomes incidental to the screening. *When* to watch matters far less than *whether* one may choose to watch in the first place.

Given that universities are, indeed, bastions of privilege, it would be simple to characterize the WCG's detractors as campus brats. Simple—and simplistic. After venting his banal condemnations, the sardonic letter-writer offered the group some arresting advice: "Think. If you had put your energy into getting better lighting on campus, or a walk-home program, or God forbid, a rape crisis or awareness centre on campus, instead of into protesting this insignificant film, perhaps some violence might have been avoided." The WCG got that message. After a few more weeks, its members decided to lobby the university for a "gender-friendly" women's centre where all students may pick up information, support a friend or read about equality.

In the "gender-friendly" department, they tried to lead by example.

Among the group's anchors was Craig Bradley, who resigned as speaker of the UPEI student council because the council refused to challenge the university administration over the reported rape. "Campus safety isn't petty," he says. "It's bettering the quality of life for all students, even men. After the alleged sexual assault happened, a guy couldn't walk across campus without being looked at like he was a certified rapist. Well, that's no good. Nobody, male or female, should have to feel under the gun every time they walk late at night with another person fifty feet away."

Armed with empathy, the WCG organized a meeting with Dr. Eliot in January. "Of course, he sat there hemming and hawing," Shelley recalls of the president's reaction to their pitch for a women's centre. But they played to his own sense of self-interested empathy, pointing out that the centre could be a perfect way to defuse campus tension and preempt future crises. "He stopped hemming and hawing, and started to listen."

At the close of the discussion, Dr. Eliot was guardedly receptive. "[H]e told us we could have a space for our 'little women's meetings'—that was the tone—but I'm sure in the back of his mind he thought, 'They'll never get their shit together and make this happen,' " Heather surmises. "Surprise!"

One month later, the WCG had put its plan on paper. To keep things reasonable, it asked to locate the centre in an old, out-of-the-way storage space. It did not ask for funding. But, Lori says, the WCG had presented the proposal as a list of "demands," language that sent Dr. Eliot into a frenzy. At the next meeting, he slammed his fist on his desk and bellowed that the students could not get whatever they wanted whenever they wanted it. Not buying the "spoiled children" charge—a proposal for a women's centre had been submitted eight years earlier and the university administration ignored it then—the WCG nonetheless figured that it needed some advocates on the inside.

Grudgingly, the group approached the head of a university task force that was established to examine campus assault. As their shared goals became clear, and mutual suspicions subsided, the task force helped the WCG acquire a phone and a carrel in the UPEI library. The aim was to improve their proposal by researching the budgets, mandates and facilities of women's centres at other campuses. Three months of study took WCG members to spring 1993—and a new, seemingly watertight request went to the administration.

This time, it worked. In spite of a few reservations, the university's governing board granted the WCG's blueprint a decent space and a small amount of funding. By September 1993, WCG members were cutting the ribbon with Dr. Eliot, who had even donated gaudy mustard-coloured couches to the new centre.

When I caught up with them a year later, the WCG had been dismantled, but its former members had not forgotten the reasons for their success. Like Nellie McClung's Political Equality League, the WCG recruited allies from all quarters, including the System, where it offered the greatest hope for results. On top of that, the WCG linked distinct agendas to a common cause—safety—which reminded everybody of their enlightened self-interest, their individual power to contribute to the cause and their responsibility for making that choice. Heather sums it up this way: "I think we became a feminist group because we chose to cooperate to improve the quality of life on campus."

She emphasizes that the group did not paint a placard that blared, STARTING A FEMINIST BRIGADE. EVERYBODY COME. "What happened was, a bunch of concerned people got together—'people' being the important word—and worked to change something. When you talk about change, you're talking about changing human lives. I don't believe you can separate men from women's lives, because we have fathers and brothers and sons and yes, even friends, who happen to be men."

That level of openness attracted Craig and kept him involved. "I believed in what they—or we—were doing. I was with the student union for a while at the University of New Brunswick, where I dealt with feminists who wanted to change every word in the dictionary. But this was different." Different not only because of the issue's relevance to the entire student population, but because the WCG showed a willingness to learn from Craig's expertise. Having been a student politician on more than one Atlantic Canada campus, he knew how to infiltrate the byzantine bureaucracies of the region's universities—a familiarity that served the WCG in its lobbying.

"Craig grounded us," Shelley says, adding that Heather's own experience in the student union made for a tight working relationship between the two troublemakers.

"Actually," Craig clarifies, "during the whole assault incident, Heather and I were getting, like, two hours of sleep a night. We were going pretty heavy on some other student union business. By the time I got to the first

WCG meeting, I was exhausted and carrying on like a fool. So I joined the group."They all burst into laughter. But they do not want a moment of self-deprecating levity to obscure Craig's feminist legacy.

"A big part of our experiences as women is not being taken seriously," Shelley says, "and he took us seriously."

Adds Lori: "He'd explain the system to us and we'd try coming up with strategies where we wouldn't lose our integrity."

Each member, then, did some bending to belong. Craig remembers warning his fellow agitators that their protest against *Cannibal Women* would call more attention to the movie than it deserved."We still disagree on the issue," Heather confesses with a devilish smirk. In dealing with the university bigwigs, too, the group jousted over when to follow the administration's rules.

"Some of us didn't want to take the time that the system takes," Lori says. "And Craig would remind us that the only way we'd get results is by putting in the time. We still didn't want to go with the system, so we'd compromise. We'd say, 'Okay, we'll go this far with your way and after that, we'll go with our way.' "

"But it was never me against them," Craig jumps in. "It was a learning process for us all." I profess skepticism, provoking Heather to respond.

"Look, there was never a time when we gave him a code of conduct. We didn't ask him to check his genitals at the door because we had a common goal and we worked together on that basis."

"Except he wouldn't come with us when we wanted to get those tampon dispensers," Lori notes mischievously.

Shelley hurries back to the point about the participation of men. "You can't effect change if you don't allow for education. As long you exclude the people you need to get to the most, the change you achieve will be pretty fleeting."Which is why, a year after WCG members opened the women's centre, their hand-written sign remains on the front door: NOT FOR WOMEN ONLY. Even so, in the centre's inaugural week a student walked in to get information for her boyfriend. He wanted to support a female friend who had just been assaulted. But, says Lori, "he didn't feel comfortable coming in because he didn't know we were gender-friendly. So he asked his girlfriend to help him help her." Old hierarchies do not die overnight. Sometimes, they grow more complex.

As such, for all of the WCG's successes, a suddenly sombre Heather wonders what has been accomplished—and what still needs to be done. "It's going to take a lot more than the Women's Constituency Group and this centre to create real change," she volunteers in a pensive tone. "Serious change depends on working as a group and how big that group is. I don't think we've affected the way people really live in this world."

"How can you say that?" Lori challenges. "Real change starts with awareness."

"That's what I mean. The start is there, but it's going to take a lot more than six of us," Heather shoots back. "A hell of a lot more."

"We're getting there," Lori assures. "Finally, people are arriving on campus during Frosh Week and saying, 'Okay, this can happen,' instead of, 'Rapes don't occur on campus; violence doesn't exist.' Every frosh now has a more honest orientation."

Craig nods. "Between the centre here and the alarms installed across campus, I think we've improved the quality of life for everyone."

In the strained pause that follows, I watch the group members. They do not fix their eyes on each other in anticipation of more pep talks. They stare out the window. Or at the floor. Or at the newborn Shelley cradles.

"That's true," Heather finally whispers in Lori's direction. "What we did might be a change for this whole province because so many people who live here have gone to this school. It's a huge part of island life and somehow we, just average, everyday students at an institution where our parents went; we, the products of their upbringing—if we believe inequality still exists, then it can't be too far from the truth. What we did is, we brought the issue home to P.E.I."

The upshot of this case is that no charge was laid. According to Barb McKenna, former crime reporter and now a columnist for the *Charlottetown Guardian*, police quietly claim that the alleged victim's evidence fell through. However, Lori speculates that by the time the young woman had a chance to tell her story, so many sides had been bandied around that the student's version conflicted—thus sounding contrived. Indeed, confusion seems to characterize much of the affair. UPEI took several weeks to verify that the file remains open. Meanwhile, nobody I talked to could remember if the woman even retracted her complaint, an amnesia that suggests this incident never entered island lore.

Still, having "brought the issue home," the WCG torpedoed any excuse that islanders might marshall to tag rape "a mainland problem," and thereby to dodge responsibility. Anne of Green Gables, the storybook spunk maiden whom islanders adore, has grown up and gone feminist.

Towards the end of our discussion, held one year after the WCG founded the campus women's centre, Heather cast doubt on how much could really be accomplished. Her doubt sprang, in part, from the palpable friction in the group. At the time of my visit, at least two members were barely on speaking terms. The interview marked their first reunion in a long while.

If emotional decompression sneaks up on most collective endeavours, too often the result is implosion. In activism as in life, our expectations of accountability demand reasonable limits. Heather believes that, despite their disagreements about strategy, members of the WCG stuck together during the height of the fight because they cared enough about the issue to be accountable to one another. The issue, then, established the parameters of their solidarity. So when the crisis faded, those parameters necessarily dissipated, leaving WCG members with differing notions of loyalty, responsibility and solidarity. After the women's centre flung open its doors, nobody from the WCG knew what more to expect—if anything. In that brittle context, a few eggshells snapped.

The details intrigue far less than the resulting questions. How much accountability can we consistently expect of each other without courting betrayal? I do not know. Perhaps, merely by being social creatures, by surrounding ourselves with others, we already chance disappointment and flirt with betrayal. A little trust will likely not worsen those prospects. But what happens when trust, repeatedly violated, can no longer be sustained? I passionately believe that walking away—as Sadia Zaman did from mainstream journalism—need not amount to an admission that values such as accountability are useless. Sometimes, saying "to hell with it" is the way to preserve integrity, also known as accountability to the self. Limiting our expectations allows us both to stay real and to move on.

Although embracing empathy, agency and accountability should not have to mean surrendering a healthy skepticism, a healthy skepticism in turn should not have to mean stifling our fantasies prematurely. So how big can we realistically dream, courtesy of these values?

CHAPTER 8

the alchemy of
democracy

"What I'm working for," says Claire Huang Kinsley, "boils down to how we as human beings deal with each other, because both our personal lives and broader social structures are the result of human interaction. I'm working towards the day when we care about one another's needs in the same way that we care about our own. For me, this has direct relevance to violence, because what does violence stem from if not the feeling that I am more important than you; that what I need is more important than what you need, so I'm just going to take it? We have to try to change this, if only for the sake of global sanity."

Adds the black belt in pragmatism, "I don't expect it to happen in my lifetime."

Intentionally or not, Claire conceives of a just society through the vocabulary of needs. That, according to Michael Ignatieff, exhibits far more realism than the lexicon of desires. In *The Needs of Strangers*, Ignatieff argues that "[t]o define human nature in terms of needs is to define what we *are* in terms of what we *lack*, to insist on the distinctive emptiness and incompleteness of humans as a species. As natural creatures, we are potential only." (Emphasis in original.) To realize our potential, we must specify what we need. But "[t]he only human goods a needs language can specify are those absolute prerequisites for any human pursuit." In other words, needs such as freedom from violence are not frivolous, gratuitous or narcissistic. We truly need them because "we can scarcely be reconciled to ourselves and to others without them."

This brings us to a paradox. Being realistic about how much we can achieve through personal values means being as ambitious as needed for human interaction. After all, human interaction is belonging's bottom line. Dana Putnam's own hopes reflect this tension between realism and ambition. "I believe there's a basic human level that everyone should be granted," she states. "All people should be heard." She stops. "You know what—it's not going to happen, is it?" She regains confidence. "I take that back; it's just complicated." Yes, it is complicated. The values of empathy, agency and accountability do not cut a clean, linear path to results. They are not a thirty-day, money-back, three-step program to social justice. I am nobody's late-night Cher.

But if we can expect complexity to muck up our ambitions, we might also *base* our ambitions on the near-magical way that these values sometimes buttress each other. To wit, empathy without agency adds up to pity. Accountability without agency makes way for guilt. And agency without accountability is something akin to fascism, often giving rise to violence. Of pity, guilt and fascism, none can be called the stuff of belonging.

No matter how revolutionary the cause. For example, agency with some empathy but no accountability produces phenomena like the Unabomber scare. Relating to the economic insecurity of others, this obscure terrorist singlehandedly stalked America's political, academic, industrial and journalistic establishment with his threats to kill airplane passengers and university faculty if newspapers did not give his anti-technology manifesto wide exposure. Over almost two decades, the Unabomber planted sixteen package bombs, murdered three people and injured twenty-three in an effort to publicize his people-first rant. His agency raged, his empathy had its limits and, by virtue of his refusal to be identified, his accountability did not exist. Neither did any lasting power.

By showing how the three values seem to need each other's reinforcement, I am getting at what I call "the alchemy of democracy." To me, the word "alchemy" connotes mystery, experimentation and the sense that, with faith and creativity, some elixir will emerge from the brew. It seems that empathy, agency and accountability coalesce into an ethos of belonging by which each of us is bound in a contract. The contractual conditions: I will bend—agency—in exchange for the right to belong—empathy. Accountability keeps us committed to the covenant. Empathy does not always lead to agency, of course, but without the former, the latter becomes less likely, which then allows us to sidestep accountability.

Democracy, it appears, is a delicate balancing act among values such as these. Belonging *needs* democracy. And it is within our power—within the scope of ambitious realism—to pursue democracy as the consummate expression of empathy, agency and accountability.

Nobody I have met confirms the possibilities of ambitious realism better than Deborah Tagornak. The twenty-six-year-old mother and youth counsellor lives in the five-thousand-person Keewatin District of the Northwest Territories—specifically Rankin Inlet, a community situated between the Manitoba border and the Arctic circle on the wind-stripped coast of Hudson Bay. Deborah's empathy with aboriginal victims of violence fosters her agency to champion changes in Inuit society; changes so necessary, she says, that they will benefit the health of every Inuk. Thus her accountability to future generations.

Among the mammoth changes that she has undertaken is to help recreate democracy in the Arctic. By spring 1999, Canada will have a new northeastern territory—Nunavut—and Deborah's advocacy, low-key in style, high impact in potential, could contribute to making Nunavut's the world's first gender-balanced parliament. "In my language [Inuktitut], Nunavut means 'our land.' The territory will belong to all of us, so we should not lose the opportunity to make our brand-new government as democratic as possible," she asserts gently, often glancing at the floor, her humbleness a neon contrast to the grandness of her dream. "All we're asking for," she says of Inuit women, "is a system of one man, one woman for each constituency that's represented."

There are hurdles. After drawn-out debate, the Nunavut Implementation Commission—a body of eight men and two women—recommended this year that the federal Liberals enact gender parity in the territorial legislature. Although Indian Affairs minister Ron Irwin supports the proposal, MP Jack Anawak, arguably the most influential Liberal from the North, resists legislating a gender balance. He wants the idea put to a plebiscite, which could ambush the local consensus negotiated by Deborah and others. Having heard the remarks of many men in her community, Deborah has reassured them that women do not want to take over; they just want to assume their rightful place beside men. At the same time, she has underscored to Inuit men that equal political participation is not a constitutional nicety. It is a living tribute to some aboriginal traditions and a practical strategy for a higher standard of life. Deborah explained in a brief delivered to Nunavut authorities on behalf of Pauktuutit, the thirteen-year-old Inuit women's association that has become a public conscience in the North:

> Inuit men and women have always worked together and our skills are complementary. In the old days, Inuit survived in a harsh environment through cooperation. The two-member constituency model has the potential of carrying on this long-standing tradition of collaboration. Today, we are more likely to be confronted with invisible and less concrete problems associated with our humanness ... Problems like suicide, family breakdown, alcohol abuse, unemployment, and loss of culture dominate our consciousness. Addressing [them] requires a different kind of strength, but we also need to utilize a full range of traditional skills, practices and values like cooperation, generosity, and fellowship.

While celebrating their relevance, Deborah does not exaggerate the egalitarian strains of her aboriginal culture. One Inuit custom, which assigns men the responsibility to hunt and thereby feed parents in their old age, stipulates that the first child should be a boy. In some areas of the Arctic, female babies were put out on the ice to die until recently, when Old Elizabeth, an elder who lost five daughters to this practice, encouraged men and women to question it. Likewise, at a 1994 workshop on self-government, Pauktuutit directors were asked to imagine their ideal communities. Among the responses: "[Safety] for women, children and elders." To that end, "Men will be more open about their feelings and [women and men] will be able to communicate with each other ... We will all communicate with our children." By the same token, "communities will have sewing centres where women can make parkas and traditional fur clothing and elders will teach young women."

If weaving the contemporary and the traditional makes sense to Deborah, it is probably because there are few static borders for her. Born in Churchill, Manitoba, she was raised in Repulse Bay, 480 miles north of her current home. Given the area's hundred-year history with traders, federal bureaucrats and Catholic missionaries, Deborah grew up charting her way through the "white" and aboriginal worlds. Although the material poverty of the region remains—most people in the Keewatin District report an annual income of less than $10,000—her personal openness shouts as boldly as the physical expanse of the Arctic. So much so that, as an adult, Deborah has ventured to cross the most entrenched boundary of all: the silence surrounding her abusive past.

"A lot of what shaped my world is that, when I was between seven and nine years old, I was molested, fondled by a close relative, a male," Deborah says. "From there, I didn't know how to explain what happened to me, because I was just a child. I started to become very angry, wanting more attention from my parents. They just thought I was a spoiled brat. Then it got worse—alcohol and drugs."

Three years ago, Deborah decided that a family member had to know about the molestation. She phoned her aunt, who instructed her to come home and tell her father. Deborah did. "Boy, was I ever humiliated," she remembers. "Never been so humiliated in my life. With my brothers and sisters, sister-in-law, aunts and uncles around me, my father threatened me with a weapon and forced me to say what happened, in detail. I could not remember too many details and I did not want to be treated that way. He scared the shit out of me."

After her father's outburst, the family held a forgiveness prayer—with a proviso. "I was told that my news should not go outside of the house, so I kept it quiet for a long time. Well, the silence worked for them. It did-n't work for me." Moreover, she could not shake off the impact of her father's fury. "That moment of humiliation changed my whole point of view on equality," Deborah says. "I thought: When someone has the guts to be honest, they should not face more violence. There should be one-on-one equality—listening, understanding, healing. After what happened to me, I knew there had to be a person saying something about violence, facing it and fighting it, for the people and for the betterment of the person herself."

In her own version of empathy, agency and accountability, Deborah developed a personal commitment to "talk, feel and trust. I think a lot of older people in my culture are saying, 'Don't talk about the abuse, don't feel anything about your past and don't trust anyone to help you.' " She calls this lack of communication "the biggest social problem we have; the secrets are just eating us as a people. Nobody's dealing with their hurt, so it comes out as violence, anger, even suicide."

As it did in her former relationship. Deborah's boyfriend of two years—whose violence bruised the three-year-old body of her daughter,

Victoria, and sometimes drove mother and child to seek overnight shelter in a jail cell—killed himself after Deborah walked out. Only later did she discover that he had toyed with suicide for ten years. He had confided nothing to her about being physically mistreated and shuffled among seven families as a child. Nor did he share the most devastating aspect of his life. "A few years ago, he found out he was the son of a rapist," Deborah explains. "That's when he got really hurt. Even then, he never talked to me about it."

Although Canada has the world's eleventh highest rate of youth suicide, the frequency with which young northern natives snuff out their lives can be many times greater, thanks in large measure, Deborah suggests, to too little expression deteriorating into too much oppression. But, she reminds me, it is an oppression under which certain choices can still be made—such as the choice not to inflict one's grown-up grief on a child. "I understand where his anger came from," Deborah says of her ex-boyfriend. "I can't excuse what he did with it."

She admits that her rejection of excuses enjoys little sympathy, and even less empathy, among native elders. "When I tried to explain my feelings about being humiliated [by her father], you know what the elders said? 'You're too young, you should not talk back.' Like, talking back and explaining something, they lumped it into one. Well, it's not the same thing. Young people are just trying to have an understanding, and if the elders expect us to understand their hardships, they have to realize that we're going through some of our own right now." That realization seems especially pressing in a region where almost 50 per cent of the population is under the age of eighteen and only 6 per cent older than fifty-five.

Ironically, Deborah invokes a positive lesson from her Christian education to bridge the suspicions between young and old. "In school we were told, 'Speak up!' When we went home it was older people telling us, 'No, you're younger than us so you should just listen.' But it's not being against your nation, your culture, to talk about the problems of your people. The youth I work with, they want to help themselves and their families because they care about the future of the Inuit."

In fact, the youth peer-support program she cofounded in late 1994 with her new partner, Bob, could barely keep up with the demand. The Kivalliq Youth Group targets those eligible to vote and attempts to meet at least three times a month. "Our goal," Deborah says, is to "empower youth to speak their minds about social issues and give them a network of friends to rely on." These friends now include elders. "I try to get them involved as well so that they can share their survival skills and knowledge of the Inuit heritage. At our first meeting for youth in Rankin Inlet, we had different generations talking about social issues for three hours! Once the communication starts, the trust builds up. That's the start of the healing process."

Deborah transfers these lessons of suicide prevention to her work with established political brokers. Her leadership sometimes strengthens theirs. In 1994, Martha Flaherty, a nationally recognized Inuit spokesperson, wrote about Deborah in anonymous yet admiring terms:

> Last year, at Pauktuutit's Annual General Meeting in Goose Bay, a young woman spoke to us about sexual abuse and the way communities can turn on victims who decide to report abuse to the police. She spoke about the lack of support and lack of understanding she encountered in the schools, the church, social services, and among Elders. She was not used to speaking in public, and it was only her conviction that something must be done about the problem that gave her the courage to speak ... This young woman's courage touched my heart. Even though she is young, I learned a great deal from her.

That meeting saw community leaders let go of their sorrow after two, three, even four decades of self-censorship. "There were lots of grieving sessions," Deborah recalls, "and not just with women. A lot of male Inuit leaders, sexual abuse victims, got a chance to talk about it."

Opportunities to heal collectively impress Deborah as the best rationale for gender parity in the new Nunavut parliament. Women's presence in the legislature could translate into a support network for men, "who need to start talking about their own experiences, especially in the residential schools." She mentions Chesterfield Inlet, a Keewatin community whose Catholic school, recently abolished, brutalized some of the children who would become today's male Inuit leaders. "I hate to say this," Deborah acknowledges, "but knowing them and watching them, I think these leaders are still blocking out a lot of their pain. Women talk about social issues, and I think that's why some of the men don't want gender equality. They're afraid of letting down their guard." At the very least, she says, a legislature half-composed of women would lift the stigma of solitary suffering.

It could also cultivate a deep understanding of the need to fund facilities such as healing houses in order to rebuild Inuit families. "Women have a better idea of this than anybody," Deborah insists. As an example, she recounts running away from a terror-filled relationship, winding up at the police station, tolerating the snickers of uniformed authorities and begging for permission to sleep with her child in a cell. Such memories can inform legislative priorities. "Instead of offenders staying at home and the victims getting out, which is what happens now, the offenders need to be rehabilitated and the victims need to heal."

Deborah concludes that a democratic Nunavut could offer "a truly new beginning for all of us in the North." The perfect end to an interview, except ...

Will she run for parliament? Deborah looks away; her shoulders hunch and an embarrassed smile creeps across her slightly rosy face. "There are no guarantees," she says coyly. I balk at her graceful evasion, a handy trait for a politician, I teasingly point out. Relaxing again, Deborah clarifies that she enjoys working directly with young people, loves spending time at home with her daughter and wants to give her new relationship a chance. Beyond that, she wants to build up strength for "a face-to-face talk with my father about what happened between us." Not long ago they spoke on the phone, "heart to heart." She says the distance helps, and that is why ensuring more honesty in person will be a challenge. "So my plate is pretty full as it is," Deborah says, affirming her hesitance to weigh it down further with a parliamentary career. "Balance is a very important thing."

She makes that point in another way. "Some people say I'm gifted in speaking in different political arenas, but I tell you: I'm not gifted; I've experienced what I talk about. I'm not trying to put myself so high, I'm not trying to be proud of it, I'm just trying to explain to them that there should be equality for the health of everyone." I ask Deborah if she is a feminist. She sits tight-lipped for several seconds, meditating, I suspect, not on her answer but on my label. In the end, she defines herself by values. "Maybe I'm a feminist, maybe I'm not. I don't know much about that kind of thing. I just know I wouldn't want my child to go through what I did."

Deborah's response reminds me of Mariam Jalabi's warning not to replace one colonialism with another in the name of progress. It is a guiding lesson for those with dreams of democracy. Both Mariam and Deborah spurn the connotations of the feminist label, instead designing their boundaries through their behaviour—and thus accepting responsibility for their choices.

Contrast this to the quirkier situations of Tzeporah Berman and Karen Pederson. Each calls herself a feminist. Each presents her battle as a struggle for the earth's survival. Each seeks to protect the land from corporate carelessness. Yet Karen's defence of the family farm is an answer not only to the "greedy" captains of industry but also to "progressive" environmentalists who attack all organized farming as a violation of nature's integrity. I can imagine how Karen would be seen as less feminist than Tzeporah, despite her voluntary assumption of the label.

Moreover, Karen's concern for being recognized as a feminist as well as a farmer mirrors Dana Putnam's concern about being acknowledged as a feminist while being a homemaker. In each patch of the feminist field, doctrine crumbles like so much parched earth.

Trudy Parsons provides other examples of strict labels unravelling; and yet, she demonstrates how difficult it can be to escape the tyranny of tags. No matter what Trudy attempts—long hair, multicoloured hats, a lowered head—she gets known for her look and her disease. No negotiation permitted.

Unsurprisingly, then, everybody on this journey has intimated, if not stated outright, that dialogue demystifies. They have also shown that values which honour dialogue afford a certain sense of personal control. Probably more than any other endeavour today, relationships offer the hope that an investment of hard work will pay off. Try saying the same about the dividends of formal study, the prospects for job security, the future of pensions.

But whether it is Thomas Ponniah launching the college semester with workshops to build student solidarity, or Nicole Soucey slowing down to learn the needs of a restauranteur, or Sadia Zaman paying extra attention to the accuracy of the images she broadcasts, real communication undermines instant gratification. More precisely, the instant gratification that marks North American culture undermines real communication.

Can the alchemy of democracy compete with the intoxicating rush of technology? Might the values of fifteen Canadians engender a mass democratic movement? A world of multiple epiphanies awaits exploration.

.III.

vision

"It's about complexity. It's about thinking differently,
thinking creatively. Now is the time for courage, for
relentlessly speaking the truth about what we
need in our day-to-day-lives."

—Organizational consultant Clarissa Chandler,
"Anti-Oppression Strategies in Times of Backlash," 1995

"A free society is not a calm and eventless place—that is
the kind of static, dead society dictators try to create.
Free societies are dynamic, noisy, turbulent and
full of radical disagreements."

—Novelist Salman Rushdie,
"How News Becomes Opinion and Opinion Off-limits,
or the Rigours of Ostrich-Farming," The Nation, 1996

CHAPTER 9

a new political culture

Thank you, feminism, but I am moving on. My feminist compass no longer suffices for this journey; influenced by my co-travellers, I am picking up a broader map to belonging.

Feminism, which brought me to this point, claims a proud place on that map. Because of the movement's cultural coups, I and many of my co-travellers have grown up expecting to be neither sculpted nor scripted. It is partly because feminism succeeded in expanding our world views that we do not fear further expansion. In that sense, we honour the movement by travelling beyond it for a more encompassing ethos of belonging.

I have long understood that belonging takes time. What my co-travellers taught is that belonging *should* take time for everybody with democratic aspirations. This is an almost blasphemous conclusion, because living in the age of instant gratification tempts all of us to seek instant justice, perverting justice into convenience. Sound bites get shorter to suit the fickle loyalties of channel-surfers, fast food chains train employees to serve customers ten seconds sooner than their rivals, and some of us stand over our fax machines cursing when our documents do not transmit in under half a minute. (Thus the "necessity" of e-mail.)

In a world where speed poses as need, even momentary pain can sweet-talk us to the status of powerless victim, convinced that without a wholesale revolution, we are left with only the choice of scrounging for refuge on the fringe. If my desires cannot be met this minute, then I am forking out too much in taxes, or you are racist, or in some other way the System has it in for us and there is no justice at all. To modify the popular activist chant: "What do we want? Belonging! When do we want it? Now!"

If we aspire to democracy, though, "Hey, hey, ho, ho, a chant like that would have to go!" This is because belonging does not roll in with the supply trucks of a liberationist army, as Cuban women realized two decades into the Castro revolution and as some Palestinians are now discovering at the clenched fists and clay feet of their own police force. Nor, then, is belonging something we can "get," however loudly we demand its delivery.

Genuine belonging starts with reasonable self-doubt. When we doubt our certitudes, we have an incentive to learn from others, who in turn can teach us about our own hidden dimensions. As the "talk" and "trust" ethos of Deborah Tagornak suggests, we begin to strip our suspicions when we risk give and take. Hers is a faith in "one-on-one equality"—transforming power through individual relationships rather than merely transferring power through mass revolution. If Deborah Tagornak is a Pollyanna, then so was Nellie McClung. Change, concluded the victorious suffragist, "seems to happen best in the context of the relationship. People are more likely to hear the prophetic word when it comes from someone they trust."

Thus, in the world to which my co-travellers have guided me, nobody is "given" justice. Everybody has the right and responsibility to bargain for it. To ensure that diversity is respected—a condition of belonging—patient negotiation must supplant instant gratification. As long as the alchemy of democracy is part of our individual constitutions, our labels will count for less than our commitment to venture beyond them.

But let us rein in the dream: that empathy, agency and accountability percolate within a few disparate people scarcely makes for a political culture. It is cause for optimism that a handful of young Canadians value diversity enough to practise democracy. What, though, of others?

Canadian pollster Michael Adams provides more optimism. In his 1997 overview of the Canadian psyche, *Sex in the Snow*, Adams writes that "new values and motivations are developing in our culture," emblematic of "a quest for meaning and a new social fabric." He depicts the post-boomers as trailblazers of a shift from the acceptance of stubborn hierarchy to the embrace of a progressive yet pragmatic outlook that oozes the potential to produce "communities of choice based on mutual interest, affinity, and need, as well as greater flexibility of personality, and even of race and gender identity."

It is as if Adams describes the lives of my co-travellers. *His* discoveries, when accompanied by *their* values, raise the possibility of an ascendant new democracy. I would call it a radical democracy.

According to philosopher Jean Bethke Elshtain, democracy "is the political form that permits and requires human freedom" for the sake of "service to others in one's own time and place." Given this interplay between liberty and responsibility, Elshtain stresses that democracy "is not simply a set of procedures [or] a constitution, but an ethos, a spirit, a way of responding, a way of conducting oneself every day." Likewise, I assess the vigour of democracy by how much we are entrusted to do as citizens—merely to cast a ballot every few years, or also to participate between elections?

Both of our conceptions emphasize constant interaction among citizens. As such, radicalism in democracy exists not on the outskirts, but at the bustling centre, of public discourse. Those who define "radical" as "being marginal" often accomplish little more than dodging their participatory responsibilities and forsaking their right to be heard. In a legislature, on campus, around the neighbourhood or at a dinner party, to be radical is to stretch towards the truths of others, particularly those who seem most unlike us. Stretching need not mean getting bent out of shape; I will only stretch so far towards anti-choice picketers before rationality tells me to recoil. But suppose a picketer is rational. Suppose he quotes not only from a biblical verse but also from a medical report, or two, or more, of which I have never heard. Then what? Then I am dared to damn my lazy desire for quick conclusions. Otherwise, what makes me more a champion of informed choice than he?

Democracy is a mammoth dare. When we graduate from staring at strangers to engaging them in argument, we have to brace for the surprises, the shocks and the myriad educational adventures in between. Until we "defend our opinions in public, they remain opinions—half-formed convictions based on random impressions and unexamined assumptions," noted the late American cultural critic Christopher Lasch. At the same time as informing ourselves, "the act of articulating and defending our views ... makes it possible for others to recognize them as a description of our own experience as well. In short, we come to know our own minds only by explaining ourselves to others." Lest we lapse into smugness, however, he warned that the "attempt to bring others around to our point of view carries the risk, of course, that we may adopt their point of view instead." Argument, Lasch reasoned, is "unpredictable," and therefore elevates democracy "not as the most efficient but as the most educational form of government."

Well and good for the chattering classes, some might sneer, but reality dictates questions like, "What would radical democracy do for the poor?" For the question of belonging to be treated seriously, it would have to address bread-and-butter injustices. To wit, Canada's two-thousand-plus food banks outnumber any one company's fast-food outlets. In addition, five firms and thirty-two families dominate a third of the country's "non-financial assets," according to the Conference Board of Canada. And among industrial countries, Canada comes second only to Australia in easing taxes on the wealthy. By comparison, Richard Gwyn writes, the elite in post-Thatcher Britain contributes twenty times more to its country's total tax take. As for the richest in post-Reagan America? Twenty-five times more.

This, it seems, is the only U.S. policy trend that has not penetrated Canada. Indeed, current Canadian solutions to the injustices above draw deep from American welfare "reforms." Mandatory workfare, for example, has popped up in provinces of diverse political stripes even though, by the findings of the Canadian Policy Research Network (CPRN), "many Canadians worry that workfare ... will breed a new form of dependency and further destroy one's work ethic and pride." In the midst of this heavy-handedness, how can I possibly believe that radical democracy might amount to more than a feel-good philosophy culminating in a national high-five? How can civic interaction be enough to subvert bad policies and inspire better ones?

Civic interaction is not enough. But as a start, it is imperative. *New York Times* columnist Anthony Lewis conveyed that message last year when denouncing a Republican bill which slashes aid to the poorest Americans and withholds cash welfare from even legal immigrants, a pre-election measure signed by President Bill "I feel your pain" Clinton. "The truth is that we do not understand [the] ills afflicting our society," Lewis lamented, "and we do not have the solutions for them. So in a piece of legislation like the welfare bill we act in ignorance and frustration." Far from encouraging us to settle for a group hug, what radical democracy can do is teach us about each other's afflictions and privileges so that public opinion has more accurate information with which to set priorities and design solutions. The CPRN confirmed this possibility when conducting its recent study *Exploring Canadian Values*. Under the heading "democratization," it notes:

> What Canadians realize, in the discussion group process, is that ... discussion of values and principles enriches understanding of social policy. Discussion enables people to work through issues in a process of developing public judgment. Public judgment is an essential step in the creation of public policy.

Moreover, by linking self-interest to a greater good through the value of empathy, radical democracy could give the powerful an incentive to push socially just policies. There are historical precedents. Automaker Henry Ford saw the need not only to pay his employees a living wage but also to hire back those workers displaced by technology, for who else would purchase and popularize his cars? Big businessmen reportedly scoffed at Ford. According to economist Jeremy Rifkin, that very arrogance fuelled the stock market crash of 1929. A lesson for today's CEOs who, in a gesture of radical democracy, might ask the people they have laid off how they plan to buy what is being produced so much more efficiently without them. Commercial interest could indeed be wrapped up in workers' well-being. Empathy would bring out that connection.

In Canada, enlightened self-interest has compelled media baron Moses Znaimer to practice a hip and entirely voluntary employment equity. Understanding that viewers will likely stay tuned when they see themselves reflected on-screen, the pharaoh of Toronto's CITY-TV has filled his newsroom-turned-studio with a rainbow of reporters: female, black and Korean anchors, a man in a wheelchair on the education beat, an aboriginal journalist sporting braids. Assignment editor Dwight Drummond (a young black man who made unwanted headlines when local police arbitrarily roughed him up) told an anti-racism forum last year that Znaimer sandwiched the station between two conventional networks because he knew that Toronto's diverse viewing audience would pause at the difference. Did it ever: of the five major supper-hour newscasts, *CityPulse* attracts the highest concentration of eighteen- to forty-nine-year-olds. Znaimer is now seeking to launch a Vancouver version.

On a much smaller scale, a landlord friend of mine draws on the values of radical democracy to advocate for rent control, a policy that benefits low-income people far more than property owners—or so we are supposed to believe. Rent control serves this landlord's interest because it smooths her relationship with tenants, which means they are likely to stick around. The tenants do not imagine behind her every move a hidden agenda to wrench more money from them, and she appreciates not having the payment hassles caused by latent suspicions. In short, this landlord claims, rent control makes her job easier by fostering an atmosphere of trust. To be sure, whether or not my friend owned property, she would support rent control. As a landlord, however, she realizes that her words will be picked up if she speaks in favour of the policy. And by recognizing her self-interest in advancing it, she has a heightened incentive to act effectively.

In big ways and small, a radically democratic society sheds light on how the fate of the marginalized is welded to that of the mainstream, making mainstream solidarity with the marginalized a matter of pragmatism, not finite altruism.

In closing the distance between individuals, radical democracy gives us all a different way to think about the poor. Right now, many conservatives do not want their tax dollars directed to low-income people, for whom they figure they bear no responsibility. On the other hand, liberals generally tolerate tax dollars going to social services, because that way nobody need shoulder personal responsibility for the unfortunates. Instead of having to know them, we can be satisfied simply to know *of* them, the result being that poor people remain enigmas. Radical democracy redefines the have-nots as those who lack the imagination to interact.

This point was recently illustrated to me at a public presentation about the future of the Left, during which a Marxist law professor and I shared the podium. One of our final questioners introduced herself as a fourth grade teacher in a West Toronto neighbourhood populated by single mothers and hungry children who need hope. What, she wondered, could she take back to them from this evening?

I talked about the street-level economic projects—formally titled Community Development Corporations—that have energized many inner-city neighbourhoods in the U.S. From the restoration of buildings to the care of children to the distribution of food, all ventures are profit-

oriented yet receive start-up subsidies from government. Most important, all flourish on grassroots involvement. I argued that such initiatives
nurture an awareness of what people can control, which promotes the
practical use of resources and lends concreteness to the theoretical cornerstone of democracy: participation. My aim, I concluded, was not to
prescribe another American solution but to confirm that, with civic inge-
nuity, some hope can be extracted from the jaws of hunger.

The professor chuckled, happy for his chance to lead me and our
attentive questioner "out of the darkness." Having already crowned me
the "embodiment of everything that's wrong with the Left," he lectured
her on "false consciousness" and the "petty bourgeoisie," threw in a reference to the "cash nexus," then urged her to watch for the imminent revolution of the burgeoning proletariat. Lumpen? Not for long.

She stopped him there. "Please," implored the teacher, "bring it down
to my level."

Exasperated, the professor sputtered the same jargon louder. He
reminded me of the local who, striving to impart his superior knowledge
to the tourist but unwilling to strive to the point of creativity, cranks up
his decibel level to get the foreigner to understand him, dammit. The
teacher did not. She sat down, shaking her head in what she described to
me afterwards as disbelief.

The anti-democratic tendencies of some who claim to work against
poverty can be seen in their disdain for needs other than the material.
Asking for hope, the teacher got humiliation. What she did not need is to
be shouted at. What her students and their families certainly do not need
is to be instructed to wait for the Revolution. In a knowledge-is-power
society, the professor's deep knowledge generated no real power—the
ability to achieve the intended result—unless, that is, he intended to
alienate our questioner. Knowledge has limited sway when devoid of radically democratic values. Well employed, fed and housed, the professor
nonetheless impressed me as the poor one.

Poorer, perhaps, than the people who hawk street newspapers such as
Vancouver's *Change* magazine. It used to be distributed to the homeless at
shelters and hostels. Approaching its sixth year of operation, *Change* magazine is sold to the general public by the otherwise unemployed. Often,
more than money gets traded when one of these papers is bought. "I love
to see the haves and have-nots meet 10,000 times a month and discuss

their differences," gushes editor Michael McCarthy. "Believe me, they discuss the issues. I get a kick out of watching vendors arguing politics with
the stockbrokers." Encounters like these are entirely in keeping with the
newspaper's stated philosophy of personal empowerment, borrowed
from Chicago community organizer Saul Alinsky:

> Self-respect arises only out of people who play an active role in
> solving their own crises and who are not helpless, passive, puppet-
> like recipients of private or public services. To give people help,
> while denying them a signficant part of the action, contributes
> nothing to the individual ... Denial of the opportunity for partici-
> pation is a denial of human dignity and democracy. It will not work.

Numbering well over a hundred around the world, street papers provide hard evidence that, at least at society's ground level, the quest to
radicalize democracy is alive. Insisting on interaction and not just trans-
action, more such projects would broaden the picture of who can be
legitimate citizens.

Noble sentiments, the Marxist law professor would respond, but selling street papers reinforces the norm of capitalist supremacy, so that the
"cash nexus" continues to drive civic worth. For ordinary folks to savour
bona fide freedom, he would thunder, we have to see ourselves not as citizens who share the rights and responsibilities afforded capitalists, but as
workers whose interests directly collide with theirs.

Granted, my schools were never those of conglomerate shareholders,
and God knows their justice system is not mine. Still, I find the citizen-
or-worker ultimatum as deadening as the neo-conservative tendency to
equate citizens with consumers. Fact is, neither the centrally planned
economy nor the free market can be relied on to promote belonging.
Economic paradigms address only what human beings need to survive,
not what we need to thrive.

They do not fathom the raw emotions behind individual compul-
sions—the pure love of their environments that keeps journalist Sadia
Zaman in the alternative media, and AIDS activist Trudy Parsons at
piddly paid contract jobs, despite sexy offers from elsewhere. Or the
spiritual appreciation of "balance" that stops youth counsellor Deborah
Tagornak from jumping into a potentially lucrative career as a member

of Nunavut's first parliament. Or the sheer awe of the land that makes young, travelled, university-educated Karen Pederson even consider tying herself down to the family farm at a time of guaranteed losses for small steads and persistent chauvinism against the women who run them.

To be metaphorical, both the vulgar Marxist and neo-conservative agendas shrink the public sphere to a grocery store. Here, the prices are set, everybody knows his or her place and the express line promises instant gratification for the Revolution's big winners. As for the losers, they will have to work harder for their supper. David Tsubouchi, the first social services minister in Ontario's Common Sense Revolution, suggested that those devastated by his welfare cuts could cope by bargaining for better food prices with shopkeepers. Buy tuna in bulk and you might just knock a few dollars off your grocery bill, he mused. Rancid logic. A group of anti-poverty activists followed the minister's advice, only to be hauled away by police.

Radical democracy expands the public sphere to a sprawling bazaar where people are expected—as citizens, not as consumers or producers—to hang around and haggle for a fairer deal on what it takes to belong. Why a bazaar? In an entirely separate context, Jean-Marie Guéhenno answers that question when he describes the bazaar's multi-voice vitality: "eloquent, not exempt from double-dealing, but never totally conflictual, between people who [know] they [will] meet again."

Most important, then, *everybody* haggles for belonging. The business executive sees her stake in conversing with the young man who sleeps atop a grate because she understands that stubborn prejudice reveals nothing to her about her world—or about herself. Any good entrepreneur, by definition, risks learning, and if knowledge is power, the "poor" and the "prominent" have some of each to exchange. Consequently, the bazaar offers no express line to citizens in a hurry, no checkout counter that serves as a duck-out counter. You cannot sprint to informed judgement.

I confess that the bazaar is far less orderly than the grocery store; swapping ideas not nearly as conclusive as dealing cash for tins of tuna. But citizenship has more contours than the ledger sheets let on. Obscuring those contours strangles the possibilities of belonging. Radical democracy enriches them, and us.

I would love to trumpet that nothing can prevent this bold, bucolic democracy from flowering. In my technicolour dreams! As I broached earlier, chief among the barriers is time—or our perception of it. As long as the dog is yelping, the week is packed and the children's lunches are not, it is a long shot that most people will spare a minute to speak to that man on the grate. They would sooner spare a dime and keep walking.

It does not help that ideological revolutionaries and their cut-to-the-chase platforms play time as a trump card. Canadian philosopher John Ralston Saul exposes this tack in his 1995 elegy for civic vigilance, *The Unconscious Civilization*:

> The recurring delusion of a safe haven ... is tied to defeating time or at least to controlling it. The whole discourse of necessity and inevitability that surrounds the ideologies—from corporatism down to the payment of the debts—is constructed around a "now or never" threat. Time, the great enemy, will defeat us if we hesitate for a moment to think or doubt. Panicked, we flee towards certainty.

This stampede towards certainty cannot be divorced from the media-mad age we inhabit. The way we treat time is tied to technology's grip on our heads and hearts. In explaining how e-mail makes it simple to start sexual liaisons, one virtual romantic told the *Globe and Mail*: "Things happen faster this way and people say things earlier than they should. It's easy to type fast, it's easy to say things to the computer screen, and it's easy to open yourself up when you want to." Snap decisions; consequences to be reconciled later.

The same potion of technological tease and ethical ease prompted me to do something about which my family should have first been consulted. In the introduction to this book, I wrote about receiving a phone call from my mother. She wanted to know how I could appear on national TV and make a disclosure that, even if it did not shame me, was sure to embarrass her. At the time, I had no answer. Upon reflection (and that is my point about technology's impact on ethics; we think much later than we should), I have determined at least part of the answer. Standing before a camera meant facing an inanimate audience. The lens does not recognize a daughter; it records a performer. Nor does the lens talk back, asking the performer to justify being there. The lens merely stares. Teased by the camera's silence, I dropped the toga of discretion and draped myself in a transparent telenarcissism. It was a giddy, willful arrogance. My adopted axiom: Out of frame, out of mind. If everybody else is out of the frame, so are their objections. The audience, their dissent and my doubts come after the deed. Meanwhile, a mother gets burned.

This lesson contains clues about the prospects for radical democracy. When fourteen-inch screens hide the nuances of human interaction and postpone the ethical challenges engendered by them, communication might *feel* easier. But, uncoupled from the thought that democracy requires, communication will be stunningly superficial and self-absorbed.

If the medium is the message, in Marshall McLuhan's overused phrase, then the simplifying sorcery of TV should be the best friend of fundamentalism. Indeed, the Common Sense Revolution's high priest, Mike Harris, has garnered the title "TV Premier" for dazzling a usually cautious electorate with pictures more than policies: a cavernous baseball stadium that he invited viewers to imagine being filled with welfare recipients, or a warehouse of VCRs, stereos and camcorders that he urged viewers to visit with their tax savings. And flashing the simple words "Quota Law" on-screen cleanly summarized Harris's otherwise sloppy case against Ontario's employment equity act. The outcome, chronicles media watcher John Doyle, is that even seasoned reporters "responded like Pavlov's dogs." Bad news for radical democracy.

Jean-Marie Guéhenno fleshes out how the fourth estate has abandoned democratic debate in our TV nations. The "principal function of the politician," he opines, "is now the professional management of collective perceptions, and through them the creation of continuity." The messenger of these perceptions is the broadcast journalist. That politicians and TV producers nourish each other can be detected in the way "television imposes its rhythm on the political debate.

> Only one topic at a time is discussed, and interest soon dissipates: rarely does news coverage spend more than a week on the same question. The politician's task is to play his part as well as he can, to be as often as possible present in the fifty-some psychodramas that fill the television screen each year.

Hence the illusion of continuity. Democracy suffers because "mistakes, like successes, are soon forgotten," eclipsed by the flash of more spectacle. TV news might be democratic by virtue of its accessibility to just about any audience, its capacity to convey the indescribable and its scam-busting use of video, but it is profoundly hostile to radical democracy in that visuals project instead of propose; they assert truth rather than suggest it. Much of what gets broadcast thus gets cleansed of qualifiers like "maybe." Perhaps the great democratic service of TV news is that it includes as many people as possible in the fabrication.

Predicts Guéhenno: "[T]he ultimate stage of democracy by media will be reached when political debate no longer has any influence on actual decisions but on the collective perception that a people has of itself." Oddly, then, although the five-hundred-channel universe will bring Earth and surrounding galaxies into our living rooms, I am not sure it will stir our curiosity to look past the front door.

Except, that is, when TV fulfills its mandate of collecting audiences for advertisers and dispatches us to the mall. According to Jim Wallis, editor of the ethics-probing magazine *Sojourners*, shopping is no longer a purposeful household task but a rote rite of citizenship. So "the issue here is deeper than greed and selfishness. Material consumption," such as slapping down five dollars for a plastic, inoperable but authentic-looking car phone, "has become the primary way of belonging." Another blow against radical democracy, which prospers on participatory, not purchasing, power.

And yet, if Marxists err in believing that it is the only means through which people will choose to participate, there can be no question that purchasing is the most *convenient* means to participate. Witness the specialty-store feminists Dana Putnam talks about. They support the Cause by consuming Bridgehead coffee and Body Shop soap—a feminism of convenience in which low-income Dana holds second-class status. Much as I would like to, I cannot disagree with Wallis's conclusion: the basic civic act of voting has been usurped by the act of shopping, with democracy "reduced to the freedom to decide"—vote, really—"among forty brands of toothpaste."

Information-sharing, too, is being converted from a civic responsibility to a commercial contract. The Public Libraries Act of Ontario refers to Toronto's chief librarian as a CEO. Small wonder: public libraries have entered the business of selling their services to "customers," and their names to corporations. Similarly, journalists, academics and bureaucrats who formerly dispensed expertise for public edification today have more profitable options—to become pundits or consultants and market their information as a meal ticket. I include myself among both the merchants and the merchandise.

In this regard, consider the strange case of Gerry Caplan. The career social democrat, self-employed commentator and publicly paid co-chair of the 1995 Ontario Royal Commission on Learning caused a stir for having requested $3,500 to discuss the commission's findings at a community forum. In the controversy's wake, Caplan waived the fee for all community groups and pinned the bad call on his booking agent. To which outraged conservatives replied: What is a public servant (to say nothing of a socialist!) doing with a private agent? The answer: Returning to his job as a self-employed commentator. Given belt-tightening by the NDP government, Caplan's contract as co-chair was not extended to cover the period following the release of his education report. As a result, commission staff rerouted inquiries about Caplan's availability to his agent. In the name of fiscal responsibility, government sent the message that even if they speak as public servants, commentators are first and foremost commodities. The odds of a radical democracy sprouting from the soil of this pay-per-viewpoint society look dim.

What, then, of democratic renewal through the electronic information highway? Not likely, predicts *Washington Post* media critic Howard Kurtz. In *Hot Air*, his 1996 analysis of North America's "talk culture," Kurtz cautions that the Internet picks up where Rush and Geraldo sign off:

> Facts are often mangled. Unfounded rumours race by at 14,400 bits per second ... [Banter] degenerates into a volley of anonymous flames and personal insults. No one need take responsibility for inflammatory remarks. The computer has made every user the star of his own talk show before a vast unseen audience linked by telephone wires.

I find this case overstated, if only because it is too soon to pronounce definitively. Tomes have speculated about the democratic potential of telecommunications technology, and I do not pretend to match the specificity of their insights. But on balance, I am wary about how far the information highway will guide us to participatory nirvana. Computers link up. Marketers network. Citizens are supposed to do much more.

Many are managing to. Some social justice groups have seized upon the Internet as a minimal-waste way of getting out "the word" and build-ing coalitions with potential allies. In the early 1990s, the Net became a bridge between New York environmentalists and Quebec's Cree Indians, partners in the fight to stop the deadly James Bay II hydroelectric project. Helped by the research of wired academics, the campaigners twice con-vinced New York state legislators to reject energy contracts from Que-bec. By fall 1994, Premier Jacques Parizeau suspended his sales pitch, arguing that the project had become uneconomical for Quebec. It remains shelved. Likewise, human rights paladin Amnesty International has harnessed the Net's multinational reach to exchange sensitive mater-ial, to organize lobbies in otherwise impenetrable regions and to make contact with dissidents. Bye-bye border guards. So long postal police. Finally, for those who have seldom sensed a bond with the surrounding universe—children with disabilities, for example—the Internet pre-empts labels. The faceless, disembodied "on-line self," in Derrick de Kerckhove's phrase, gets judged for what it says and how it looks.

By the same token, being quarantined behind a computer screen will not eradicate the impulsive prejudices of the flesh-and-blood world, prej-udices that invariably infect the messages and graphics flashed on the Net. If we feast on kiddie porn in the privacy of our bedrooms, we will prob-ably give it our anonymous business on computer billboards. If we are anti-Semites around the kitchen table, chances are that we will not turn away from swastikas in cyberspace. One need only remember the overtly supremacist e-mail messages sent to me by some viewers of my TV debates. Although our physiologies do not appear on-line, that scarcely means they are irrelevant; as long as physiology matters in the real world, we will bring to the keyboard sensibilities that reflect our real-world experience with prejudice—and with privilege.

The entrenchment of prejudice and privilege is all the more probable where access to the Net comes into play. The information highway will not democratize the lives of those who cannot afford a computer, let alone the fees to log on. According to an October 1996 report by Statistics Canada, the well-to-do in this country are five times as likely as low-income people to have a home computer: 54 per cent compared to 11. On the literacy front, too, the gap glares. In a September 1995 study by StatsCan, 86 per cent of families earning over $100,000 claimed computer proficiency; only 28 per cent of the under-$20,000 crowd could do the same.

All of which suggests that some hierarchies will solidify as other hierarchies are softened, illuminating the paradox of Internet democracy. Cruising the information highway reflects a state of communication in which the world is at once there and not there, individuals social and asocial, human beings connected and disconnected, trying to court each other without bothering with any palpable contact.

Not even on-line cafés provide actual connections to a place of belonging. Clifford Stoll, the original computer geek and author of the 1995 hit *Silicon Snakeoil*, suggests that on-line cafés promise less to the computer-savvy companion-seeker than conventional singles bars. "You sit at a table and talk over the Internet Relay Chat, read Net news or play Netrek. What a lonely way to spend an evening—surrounded by people yet escaping into distant conversations." Lonely, especially, if you are attempting to attract men, who tend to be the Net addicts.

As the owner of several computers, Stoll has a quasi-marital commitment to them that mirrors my own dysfunctionally torrid love affair with TV. And yet, we sense that each medium nurses shallow relationships. If we are right, the multimedia age could cement the very opposite of radical democracy—identity politics. What I mean is, despite the hype about mass communications merging disparate lands into a global village, such technology has so far produced an environment in which human beings do not have to deal with each other really, only virtually. The same dynamic occurs in the most extreme incarnations of identity politics. There, people content themselves with relating to each others' externalities rather than burrowing beneath the labels for a solidarity of spirit.

I have not come fully to terms with whether technology will let radical democracy emerge. But I do know that the speed at which technology is advancing impells us to use its creations almost uncritically. That, in turn, sets the pace and quite possibly the principles for interaction in our off-line lives. Which is why, to take democracy any further, we need to step back and reboot our human selves. It can be done. At this moment, the Internet is not so dominant a means of disseminating information that henceforth every poignant idea, every worthy response to what ails the human condition, must submit to the Net's power. Its use grows by leaps and bounds, but we have time to adapt new technologies to democratic values. We are still capable of making radical democracy the ethical norm.

Public schools could be the places to start. Obvious reasons include the fact that history has shown classrooms to be conduits of values, that schools themselves are ripe for a rediscovery of purpose and that a society which upholds education as its politic cannot fail to make the school a locus of democracy. But to my mind there is a better reason to view the public classroom as an incubator of radical democracy: the relationships between teachers and students, and between students and students, can be models of civic interaction.

I understand that education takes place in all sorts of relationships— parent-child, minister-parishioner, and so forth. Still, these do not test democracy like relationships in the school. Parents are bound to their children by the natural ribbons of genetics and kinship, ministers to their congregations by the familiarity of a shared divinity. But teachers and students come together more or less as strangers. They enjoy no guarantee of eventual affinity. Moreover, their relationships encapsulate the hierarchies of society; power imbalances exist not only between teacher and student, but also among students. The question becomes: How do you distill radical democracy from relative hierarchy?

Former elementary school teacher Neil Postman sketches some scenarios in his captivating 1995 book *The End of Education*. (By "end," the New York University communications professor means the purpose, not the completion, of schooling.) In one radical scenario, Postman has teachers spend at least a semester instructing a subject they are not used to—particularly one that they did not enjoy or excel at in school. That way, they would be transported into the seats of most students. "When teachers returned to their specialities," Postman envisions, "it is possible they would bring with them refreshing ideas about how to communicate about their subjects, and with an increased empathy for their students."

Another of Postman's proposals for interaction would see the teacher stand before the class at the beginning of each course, admit to being fallible and challenge students to catch his routine mistakes. But students must substantiate their challenges, citing other sources and, where they can, coming up with alternate renditions of the teacher's lesson. These fuller challenges would be presented at the class's next gathering, giving students time to prepare for intellectual defiance. Aware that "getting" the teacher intellectually just does not thrill students as it might have in the past, Postman suggests that teachers arouse the self-interest of students by basing some of their marks on this rigorous pursuit of error. To balance self-interest with classroom solidarity, individual risk with peer support, the teacher would urge students to work collectively in informal consultation or in formal study groups. It is a pragmatic appeal. The more students involved in the challenge, the more who stand to gain credit, and the less sweat for each contributor.

Infusing the classroom with a participatory spirit could make students conscious players in a deeply democratic story. Postman narrates it this way: "The history of learning is an adventure in overcoming our errors. There is no sin in being wrong. The sin is in our unwillingness to examine our own beliefs, and in believing that our authorities cannot be wrong." In arguing for education by argumentation, Postman is delineating the radically democratic bazaar, robust with voices that haggle, but voices that also know what deserves to be haggled about. This approach to education, Postman writes, "holds out the hope for students"—and, I would add, teachers—"to discover a sense of excitement and purpose in being part of the Great Conversation."

Best of all, it sustains that hope in the seemingly poorest, most disadvantaged schools: those on the sidelines of the high-tech parade. Clifford Stoll affirms that there is no computer substitute or satellite surrogate for "a solid grounding in the essentials: reading, getting along with others, training in civic values." These, he believes, come from studying in the "same room" as peers, under "a fired-up teacher" who "can convey method as well as content." To the skeptical reader, Stoll issues a dare: "Name three multimedia programs that actually inspired you. Now name three teachers that made a difference in your life."

Here, however, is the rub. Bringing radical democracy into classrooms might restore meaning to public education; it will not immediately pacify the wailing that schools are "failing the grade." From what I can make of it, this wail is less concerned with creativity than control. "Who's in charge?" parents demand to know. "Is it teachers or students?" The implicit dualism of that question constricts the kinds of answers they hear—and want to hear. But what does it matter that the teacher is in charge if she abdicates her judgement to textbooks and technology? In a radically democratic classroom, the teacher sets the tone, yet it is the ethos of belonging that disciplines *her*. Individuals exercise their right and responsibility to participate, even (or especially) when that means arguing with the teacher. As

Postman reminds us, "We know what happens when argument ceases—blood happens." In that light, an effort to build community seems a more effective educational aid than is strict control.

Everyone knows Neil Postman to be a bit of a Luddite, but what of my nostalgia? It is Formica-thin, rest assured. My dream is not a democracy of the past, when city-states and pioneer hamlets proved small enough to circumscribe, then enforce, people's daily duties to one another. For one thing, the "democracies" of the classical Greek philosophers and early American republicans were, in fact, oligarchies. They flourished on the backs of slaves, restricting influence to an unusually heterogeneous group of white, male landowners. If my dream turns back the clock at all, it does not regress that far!

The language of democracy does harbour historical baggage. Solidarity, responsibility and community might have centuries-old connotations, but their implications are very now. These concepts scream for adaptation. Likewise, the term "radical democracy" did not germinate in my post-modern pituitary gland. Economist Cy Gonick attributes the phrase to U.S. sociologist Stanley Aronowitz. Gonick, a notable of Canada's old Left, goes on to describe radical democracy as "fundamental reform in the way authority is structured, building as much direct participation as possible in the institutions of everyday life and, at rock bottom, making decision-makers accountable to all those affected by their decisions."

In contrast, my adaptation of radical democracy emphasizes the individual infinitely more than the institution. Even in the public school, it is the one-on-one relationship, not the curriculum, on which I fasten. That focus on the personal relationship is intentional. The age of solid institutions, from the family to the company, has died. In trying to update the concept of radical democracy, I treat it as a set of values that takes root with the individual and radiates out.

To be sure, institutions such as corporations will be among us for a while. But will they be *with* us? Lewis Lapham, the erudite editor of *Harper's* magazine, has mused that company headquarters might replace the traditional town square. "A company like Chase Manhattan or IBM now employs as many people as lived in 14th-century Florence," he recently remarked. "That's a small city-state. And that city-state is the one that's going to give you your life, meaning, health insurance, country-club membership, pension, place in society, expense account and so forth." I respectfully disagree. Few of us rely on corporate fidelity any more, fewer still on the concept of company as caretaker. As offices downsize and more of us turn to self-employment, I believe the prospects for daily democracy will shift to the self. That is not because we define ourselves only as workers—most of us do not—but because this is an age when institutional uncertainty exports the burden of democracy to that arena which we can directly influence: our individual constitutions and thus our one-on-one relationships.

I see nothing hostile to progress in paving this transition with a cooperative, rather than a competitive, individualism. If political nostalgia dwells anywhere, it is in competitive individualism, a late-nineteenth-century creed better known as survival of the fittest and resuscitated by late twentieth-century neo-conservatives. According to this creed, the optimal way for the "weak" to get fit is that society throws them in the water and turns its head while they flap and flail. Those who work hard enough at their strokes will emerge primed. It is each drownee for himself. Not so in cooperative individualism, which works towards an elastic equilibrium between personal control and the need to look outside of our immediate worlds. Pollster Michael Adams has noticed just such a spirit pulsating in many young Canadians today—"post-individualism," by which "experience-seeking connections are more important than the mere assertion of autonomy." Whatever the label, it is through malleable relationships that this individualism gets things done.

That includes reforming institutions through relationships. Michael Ignatieff makes this point poetically when he demonstrates why belonging is too complex to be wholly addressed by more social programs and well-meaning policies:

> Giving the aged poor their pension and providing them with medical care may be a necessary condition for their self-respect and their dignity, but it is not a sufficient condition. It is the manner of the giving that counts and the moral basis on which it is given: whether strangers ... get their stories listened to by the social worker, whether the ambulance man takes care not to jostle them when they are taken down the steep stairs of their apartment building, whether a nurse sits with them in the hospital when they are

frightened and alone. Respect and dignity are conferred by gestures such as these. They are gestures too much a matter of human art to be made a consistent matter of administrative routine.

Here, again, the one-on-one relationship reigns. Individuals must perceive that they are cared about before they can return a sense of caring to their institutions. Belonging, then, does not follow from the legitimacy of certain structures; institutional legitimacy follows from an ethos of belonging.

As radical democrats invite themselves into public institutions, those institutions will be pressured to change because—recall Claire Huang Kinsley—what are institutions, structures and systems if not the formal products of human interaction? Revolutionaries, both conservative and alternative, sermonize that the System has a life of its own; overthrow it to reform it. True, I cannot forget the struggles awaiting women who have broken through the glass ceilings of exclusionary institutions. After shattering the glass, they have often wound up on their ass. Systemic power exists; however, it is not a totally faceless force. As my stories of the breakthrough women also revealed, systemic power is fed largely by individuals who choose not to support change, especially where incomes, status and egos are concerned. Democratizing the culture of an institution consequently requires more than one person to embrace the values of empathy, agency and accountability. The breakthrough women showed that if one's compromises are not met in kind, systemic change will be a chimera. Institutional reform takes at least two people—a relationship—because reciprocity in values is radical democracy's best enforcement mechanism.

Throughout this chapter, I have praised radical democracy not as a compassionate safety net, nor as a series of Yes/No referenda, but as a culture of interaction that spawns flexible civic relationships. Without firm territorial and institutional borders, though, what are we citizens of? Exactly what republic can radical democrats represent? And who would want live there?

CHAPTER 10

imperfect utopia

Welcome to the Utopia of Complexity. We are entering a society that recognizes its complexity—and revels in it. Less a state than a state of mind, the utopia can live within each of us, and when it does, we will live in a virtual nation governed by an ethos of belonging. This ethos jubilates in small differences, a celebration motivated by pragmatism. Empathy, for example, is easier when we know ourselves to be different from others. If we pursue complete conformity, it becomes difficult and pointless to imagine why someone has needs that we might not have considered important. At the same time as we rejoice in small difference, then, our common culture of interaction drains difference of the narcissism that promotes withdrawal into the self. More a notion-state than a nation-state, the Utopia of Complexity is the republic into which I usher radical democrats.

Utopia, I know, has a bad rap. Describing the weirdness of contemporary times, Canadian cultural diviner Arthur Kroker says that the "technological experience is both Orwellian and *hopelessly* utopian." (Emphasis mine.) Caroline Ramazanoglu associates utopia not only with hopelessness but with irresponsibility, too. In *Feminism and the Contradictions of Oppression*, she warns that women "cannot afford to be utopian" in the midst of "economic crises, sectional and international violence, the growing poverty and indebtedness of much of the third world, environmental disaster, and the prospect of nuclear pollution and war." Sure, when you put it that way.

Above all, Roseanne Barr makes utopia sound pathetic. "We're not in a perfectly feminist world and we never will be," sniped TV's domestic dominatrix in a 1993 interview with the *Ladies' Home Journal*. "And even if we were, I'd still have plastic surgery. It makes you feel really good about yourself ... [Mine] was like erasing years of abuse that I've done to my body. I feel like I'm starting over." Democracy, however, is no face lift. A society that strives for belonging does not hide its layers; it resolves to listen to the wisdom embedded in every wrinkle, whisker and wart.

Ambitious? Undoubtedly. Utopian? Probably, but without the drive for perfection. After all, radical democrats go out on a limb to discover others. Because their search for education does not stop, neither does the development of democracy. Nor is this utopia wholly fictitious. I believe that what already occurs in pockets can occur in spades, and the Utopia of Complexity does appear in pockets— namely, in the lives of my co-travellers. They repudiate the purse-lipped, ideological puritanism of conventional utopias, testifying instead that reality and radicalism can share a bed.

To wit, suppose that it is sweet, singing sex we are seeking from a utopia. In the world to which my co-travellers have led me, every sexual union would not rock. But as a utopian, I can envision many more sexual unions not being banal, awkward or downright tragic. Better sex for all of us? Yeah, possible. Barn-burning sex for all of us? Yeah, right. Around the globe, around-the-clock barn-burning sex would require either coherence from the human condition or the micromanagement of people's lives. The first does not exist; the second should not exist. As Dana Putnam sighs, "It's just complicated," and anybody who does not come clean about that fact is a fool, a propagandist, or both.

Will we edit out the complications or will we have the courage to draw from them all the lessons they offer? Put another way, will we sink to a place where we break windows because we have nothing to lose, or will we break bread with each other in an effort to ensure that negotiation is a choice still open to us? This utopian proposes maturing gracefully. True freedom respects the messiness of the human condition, and since our lives spill over with messiness, and since utopias make the best of what we have, my utopia would turn complexity into a virtue.

I can think of no collectivity better suited to the experiment than Canadians. In the first place, ours is a heritage of experimentation. It is because the Fathers of Confederation resisted prevailing economic wisdom, bucking the north-south pull of the American continent to carve out a country along the east-west axis, that Canada can be found on a map today. During the 1988 free trade showdown, conservatives brilliantly bottled and sold the value of experimentation by snubbing a century of their own political wisdom and telling Canadians that there is no such thing any more as an unthinkable thought. Strictly speaking, they were correct.

But without counter-experimentation, cautions Richard Gwyn, Canada might coast to oblivion. "As an invented nation, either we reinvent our traditions of egalitarianism and liberalism to accommodate the realities of today's global economy or, some year, some decade, we will simply fade away." His either/or fallacy notwithstanding, Gwyn rightly suggests that counter-experimentation will have to be cultural and psychological more than economic. That is to avoid becoming

> the national equivalent of a condominium apartment building in which owners and tenants greet each other politely and warmly, and periodically deal sensibly with common practical concerns like maintenance and landscaping, but have no sense of belonging to an enterprise with values and purposes larger than their individual self-interests.

Rather than giving Canada a new bottom line, more experimentation will have to cultivate an overarching ethos of belonging.

Necessary it might be, but are Canadians willing? Evidently so. "Canadians want to renovate the social contract," observes Judith Maxwell, president of the Canadian Policy Research Network (CPRN). The CPRN's 1995 study, *Exploring Canadian Values*, found that fiscal responsibility and self-reliance cohabit in the Canadian soul with democracy, compassion, equality and collective responsibility. Reducing the friction between these clusters of principles calls for creativity and negotiation. Canadians, the study concludes, "are able to imagine repairs, renovations, restructuring, and prefer those to the dismantling of social programs. Building a new social contract will require a more holistic approach," whereby elite privileges and not just social programs are put "on the table for trade-off." Maybe most important, "we want to be involved in the renovation process."

Michael Adams confirms the Canadian will to participate. "The kind of authority that gains respect today is not based on fear, intimidation or guilt," his surveys reveal, "but is more voluntaristic and consensual. Not chiseled in marble, but flexible." Flexibility is now "more authentic" to Canadians than rigidity.

Besides the necessity and the willingness, Canadians have a capacity for communication that will not let us despair—another dimension of our readiness for the Utopia of Complexity. Significantly, "[w]e're the most heavily cabled country in the world, and the most compulsive makers of long-distance calls," chronicles Richard Gwyn. "It's said that on arriving at the Pearly Gates, all Canadians automatically follow the sign pointing to 'Seminar on Heaven and Hell.' " In other words, we listen. And occasionally, we hear. Whatever the latest stains on its human rights record, Canada remains a remarkable example of common purpose amid competing interests, be they regional, religious, linguistic, ethnic or class. No other collectivity on earth can claim so much cohesion within so much tension.

Where else can a separatist party be legally elected to the supreme legislature of the land, with enough seats to swear the oath as "Her Majesty's Loyal Opposition," fight for the sovereignty of one province with the funds provided by taxpayers of all provinces *and* act as the most vociferous parliamentary voice to preserve national social programs? It is barely conceivable. It is Canadian.

Where else can First Nations chiefs put the minister of Indian Affairs on the hot seat for showing up at their 1996 annual meeting late—even though he had just come from fulfilling a long-standing federal promise to move one of Canada's poorest aboriginal communities, the Innu of Davis Inlet, to a less isolated location? Where else could the minister be booed after also committing to accelerated land claim talks with the Labrador Innu? Perhaps achieving all of this during the time of the Assembly of First Nations gathering was a government strategy calculated to keep the minister away yet make the biggest splash. Still, the timing coincided with a deadline imposed by the Labrador Inuit Association, whose president threatened that without progress on land claims, mining of aboriginal territory would come to a halt. Where else would such a threat be peaceably accepted? The minister's response is by no means enough, but neither is it callous indifference.

That Canada was the world's first country to enact multiculturalism does not surprise. Yet who else has a multiculturalism policy that, at rock bottom, trusts people to make nice with each other? It is flawed, but it is a faith in our readiness to accommodate that I am not sure could be felt of any other citizenry.

We can take issue with the nuts and bolts of the UN Human Development Index, which for two years running has ranked Canada as the world's top spot for men, close to top for women. More compelling, I think, are the nakedly subjective judgements from abroad. Canada, a Mexican diplomat has said, is "the solution looking for problems." American actress Jane Fonda seems to agree. Her struggle to belong in the U.S., from being excoriated as a communist for her friendship with the North Vietnamese to being branded as a sell-out for her marriage to billionaire Ted Turner, seeps into her statement that "[w]hen I'm in Canada, I feel like this is what the world should be." If anyone can approach the ideal of interactive complexity, it is us.

So how might the Utopia of Complexity differ from the Canada we now have?

To begin, revolutionaries would be exposed for what they are: glorifiers of simplicity. Invoking the late theorist of totalitarianism, Hannah Arendt, Jean Bethke Elshtain notes in *Democracy on Trial* that " 'those who went to the school of revolution learned and knew beforehand the course a revolution must take' "—namely, "centralize power, enhance the police [and] create a layer of spies and functionaries." The Bolsheviks of a bygone era leap to mind, but so do today's conservative gladiators.

Hail the Common Sense Revolution of Ontario Premier Mike Harris. Disgruntled by the centralization of power, one of the government's own members chastised Harris for launching a "new revolution" with the "old imperialism." According to MPP Morley Kells, the premier's advisors wasted no time in demanding "slavish adherence to their tight direction," so that "the prime operators have access to [MPPs] but the reverse is not true." Kells, a backbencher and veteran conservative, was brushed off as having an axe to grind because he did not make cabinet. But months after scoffing at his charge of imperialism, the government adopted a bill changing dozens of laws in one fell swoop and awarding itself the authority to skirt debate on future moves. Hence the first assignment from the school of revolution: in the name of populism, concentrate control.

As for enhancing police, the second route of revolutions, the Harris government sanctifies law and order. One of the more bizarre illustrations involves Canada's prima ballerina, Karen Kain, who showed up at the Ontario legislature with bags of petitions to protest arts funding cuts and was turned away at the door by security guards. To be sure, this happened at a time of high anxiety—the week after a mass riot on the legislature steps, when protestors and police billy clubs slam-danced. But let us grab perspective. When someone who floats on stage for a living is deemed a security threat, barred from the most public of Ontario's buildings and prevented from presenting a placid, if innocuous, symbol of democratic protest, then law and order collide with political accountability. In a revolution, we know which wins.

And the third feature of revolutions—a layer of spies and functionaries—could be the best way to characterize Ontario's burgeoning welfare cop bureaucracy. Measures include a public hotline for snitching on suspected social assistance cheaters as well as the reintroduction of random home inspections. Similar paths have been trodden in the proclaimed revolution of Alberta Premier Ralph Klein, who taught Harris to "go fast, hit hard and don't blink." Sounds like the drug trafficker tutoring the coke craver on the most efficient way to snort.

In their own predictability, to say nothing of the freedoms they snatch from civil society, revolutionaries restrict the range of human experiences. They do so because everything in their environment must be immediately clear to them, encouraging what George Grant, a Canadian conservative of days past, once feared: "decisiveness ... at the expense of thoughtfulness." In my lingo, that translates into instant gratification at the expense of negotiation.

The Utopia of Complexity would also foster a more honest Left, and I do not speak only of the old guard. Two years ago, a Toronto radio station whose motto earnestly enthuses "in love and struggle" saw in-house protests over harassment, managerial denials, staff resignations and an out-of-touch board. One of that battle's victors, a young station manager and professed "radical lesbian of colour," described her departed colleagues in us-versus-them language. "There's an element at the station operating from a very simple notion of inclusion," she told a journalist, "whereas what we've talked about is those voices that provide the most in-depth and critical analysis [and] the most cutting-edge cultural expression, which are not necessarily going to be inclusive of everybody."

Pardon me? Switch the subject from *your* alleged harassment to *their* "simple" analysis, then turf those whom you declare are not cutting-edge or in-depth enough. Strikes me as an even simpler notion of inclusion.

In the same week, the International Women's Day march wound its way through Toronto's core. What I witnessed bucked me up—men. More, in fact, than I had ever seen participating at one of these gigs. Still, most activists seemed stuck in the groove of their slogans, fastened to familiar friends, oblivious to the not-so-familiar. Attached to nobody's banner, one couple, newborn slung over Dad's shoulder, waited quietly on the corner of Bloor and Yonge streets as the rowdy crowd plastered the Royal Bank with psychedelic stickers shrieking, "Stop the Cuts!" When the march resumed, the family slipped anonymously back into the stream of consciences. Surrounded by hundreds, they nonetheless walked alone.

Two weeks later, young and old congregated at a public forum about "Anti-Oppression Strategies in Times of Backlash." The flyer advertising it was widely distributed at the International Women's Day festivities, which meant everyone there would have been welcome here. But people of colour made up the overwhelming majority of audience members— maybe because the panelists were "of colour." I cannot help wondering whether more white women and men would have attended had they readily identified with the speakers. I wonder especially about the low turn-out of white feminists: two of the three publicized panelists were well-known feminist women. Women of colour, yes, but women nonetheless. This being an "anti-oppression" forum, both talked about sexism in the same breath as racism. Is it that many white feminists who received the flyer did not consider themselves "oppressed"? Or, more likely, did they feel as if no place for them existed in a gathering that they anticipated would be mostly non-white?

Doubtless, despots of colour can intimidate all hues of humans into keeping their distance. But judging by the healthy presence of men at the International Women's Day rally, the politics of polarity cannot be defeated with continued polarity. Even if women of colour were sure to benefit more from the anti-oppression forum than white women, do the white feminists who stayed away really believe that they have no stake in propelling the freedom of others? Are they not, as the same feminists so often ask of men, part of the solution?

Feminism in the Utopia of Complexity would summon a plurality of thought because, like utopia itself, equality is an unceasing, imperfect project at the very least defined by the liberation of human potential. This means elites fluctuate, and creativity rather than ideology determines the composition of those elites. In the absence of a societal commitment to creativity, old dogma is left to learn new tricks, repackaging power without ever redistributing it.

Thus the "in-depth" simplicities of the radio station manager in my earlier story, a Brahmin of the Left whose effusions against elitism are as hypocritical as they are sophomoric. Staid ideology in one quarter legitimizes it in another. Thus also University of Toronto psychologist John Furedy, snorting that feminists who take issue with him "can stay the fuck out of my classroom." Furedy made this declaration at a conference of the Society for Academic Freedom and Scholarship. The conference was organized by Vancouver's Fraser Institute, a neo-conservative "think" tank whose head deems public interest groups "fiscal termites in the ship of state" but defends his own group's charitable tax status. Not long after the conference, Furedy became president of the Society for Academic Freedom and Scholarship. Small wonder that Robert Hughes, in his 1994 book *Culture of Complaint*, describes ideological polarization as "the crack of politics." It is damned addictive.

Heirs to a tradition of dignified compromise but increasingly surrounded by havens of anti-democratic insipidness, Canadians could use the relative sanity of a Utopia of Complexity. So, for example, rather than ordering students to drop the class if they do not like the reading list as is—an ultimatum my girlfriend got after pointing out the absence of female authors in a history course at the University of Toronto—professors can encourage students who take academic freedom seriously by circulating optional reading lists made up of students' suggestions. On today's campus, it seems, that is enough to qualify as radical democracy.

Neighbours need similar gestures of creative coexistence. Instead of summoning the moving trucks upon sighting too many of "those" people on "our" block, instead of plucking our children off the street because the new kids speak Chinese, instead of fuming that "their" higher grades jeopardize the university spaces supposedly reserved for homegrown students—but a few cries of the Coming Doom now ringing throughout suburban Vancouver—citizens in a Utopia of Complexity aspire to a mentality, not rest easy with a policy, of multiculturalism.

This highlights a concrete distinction between the Utopia of Complexity and contemporary Canada. In Canada, the language of official multiculturalism is so unquestioningly affirmative that it can mask differences within communities. Far better to acquaint each other with differences than to dictate, as official multiculturalism does, that we accept "the other" as if it is a homogeneous mass of benign foreignness. Making nice does not last. Neither does acceptance rooted in assumptions; it is not informed acceptance. In a Utopia of Complexity, multiculturalism's premier lesson is that we are persons before we are political statements, individuals before groups, diverse in our capacities, human in our foibles, entitled to having each acknowledged.

Being acknowledged is not the same as being validated. At the heart of my utopia would be the recognition that validation takes a back seat to communication. Here, people may express the scope of who they are. Here, those who express themselves are listened to. But here, they are not always agreed with. The trade-off works because being listened to means being acknowledged, the mark of having arrived as a person. Most of us would not need to exaggerate our pain if we could negotiate the contract that citizens enjoy in a Utopia of Complexity: I take the initiative to communicate my experiences to you; you acknowledge me as the aggregate of those experiences, not just the ones that you immediately comprehend. Disagree with the morals of my stories but do not dismiss the stories; you might discover something about yourself from them. In a Utopia of Complexity, there is a new definition of patriotic duty—to explore ambiguity rather than to quash it with unswerving criteria of truth.

I can hear the argument that a Utopia of Complexity would fast collapse because society needs fixed criteria as litmus tests of achievement. My detractors could point to me as proof that even unfair rules and alienating conventions have value. Without the childhood insecurity fed by my classmates chanting, "Ink, pink, you stink," I would not have been compelled to push myself beyond mediocrity. But the resentment that energized me to "prove" myself has enervated many others, most of whom we might never know about because they will not have achieved in the "proven"—read conventional—manner. The litmus test argument assumes that the vast majority of human beings have little capacity for creativity, an assumption that similarly girds uneasiness about employment equity. Because we can achieve only in selected ways, the assumption goes, we deserve acknowledgement only under tightly controlled circumstances. Merit, narrowly defined, is thus narrowly measured. Such simplicity caps human potential at its source. As journalist Sadia Zaman attests, her confidence often needs nourishment from her husband, Neil. His faith in her capacities clears room for her efforts—and subsequent achievements.

I am not advocating a world without shared standards, where criticism is muzzled and failure disguised in deference to self-esteem. In the Utopia of Complexity, everyone cannot be an elected politician, a busy plumber or an anthologized poet. If everybody is great, then nobody is. For a few years, I tried my hand at love poems, hated the delicate emotional excavations and churned out garbage. Nudged by repeated failure, I moved on to something that sparks my creativity—concocting Top Ten lists for my girlfriend. Are Letterman gags more my style of romantic subtlety than haiku? Pitifully, yes. So I am the first to say that standards count.

It is gauging greatness with reductionist standards that makes a sham of creativity, of complexity and, in the end, of democracy. Why did the media brand former NDP leader Audrey McLaughlin "weak," but Reform Party leader Preston Manning "refreshing," when both refused to bang on their desktops for publicity? Think, too, of Sunera Thobani, the first president of the National Action Committee on the Status of Women to hail from outside of central Canada—Vancouver, to be precise. In a country as racked by regionalism as ours, why was she dogged by the question, "Does NAC represent 'mainstream' women?" instead of, "Does NAC represent women east of the Rockies?" (Why should she get even *that* question?) On the other side of Canada is AIDS activist Trudy Parsons. Why have the media judged her credibility more by her looks than by her conduct? And why have some feminists done the same to Afra and Mariam Jalabi, the hijab-wearing sisters?

A world that finds worth in variety is a world that nurtures new contributions and tastes their unexpected benefits. Just ask the Brodies, the most expressive neighbours my family ever had. Taking advantage of their physical proximity to us, the Brodies salivated aloud whenever my mum grilled masala chicken on the barbecue. Because she could not unscramble a word of their Scottish brogues, Mum drafted my sisters and me to decipher on the spot. Seeing us at the fence, the Brodie kids joined in. The masala chicken meeting thus became a family affair. Our neighbours walked off with sizzling samples and we with a sense of having earned their appreciation.

Since then, our families socialized beyond the back yard, so I never felt that the Brodies had reduced us to our spice racks that day. Rather, they cared enough to ask what they were smelling. Had they asked because they despised the masala's pungency, I still think my family would have wanted the opportunity to respond. Their stewing in silence would have reinforced our invisibility, as if we were not worth the conversation—or the confrontation. In a Utopia of Complexity, people take deeper breaths, open their windows as well as their imaginations and investigate before linking pungency to filth. "Sometimes it's the contemplating silence that kills," affirms Afra Jalabi about the icy gazes she gets from fellow feminists. Do not scurry behind the invisible veil of suspicion, she urges them. Ask me questions; that way, I can answer your assumptions. Her utopia, like mine, would replace prejudgement—or prejudice—with what she calls "informed judgement."

Author Jonathan Rauch anticipates danger in the campaign to defeat prejudice. His eloquent 1995 *Harper's* magazine essay "In Defense of Prejudice" contends that "[a]n enlightened and efficient intellectual regime lets millions of prejudices bloom, including many that you and I may regard as hateful and grotesque." The genius of intellectual pluralism "lies not in doing away with prejudice and dogma" but in "making them socially productive by pitting prejudice against prejudice, dogma against dogma, exposing all to withering public criticism." Otherwise, "stamping out prejudice really means forcing everyone to share the same prejudice, namely that of whoever is in authority."

Rauch and I agree on the social productivity of an "enlightened" public sphere; we part company where he also pursues an "efficient" one. I favour public debate that is educational, and the difference between education and efficiency has profound implications for enlightenment itself. Radical democracy requires effort to convert impressions into ideas. Efforts sometimes fail. Efficiency does not tolerate much failure. The democracy Rauch depicts—misconception meets misrepresentation greets distortion—takes no effort at all. What myths are ever clarified by this efficient clash of myth-manufacturing fundamentalisms, I cannot explain.

Hence, although he paints prejudice as the telltale sign of intellectual pluralism, Rauch misses the delicious irony: that prejudice itself is anti-intellectual. It does not unleash ideas so much as it padlocks minds with the clamp of impressions. To be prejudiced is to reach conclusions before engaging in any meaningful way with "the other." To engage in a meaningful way is to exchange facts, interpretations, feelings and yes, ideas. Virulent prejudice preempts such an exchange by decreeing preconception, not engaged intellect, as the chief pilot. And if an exchange does finally follow, the presence of virulent prejudice makes that exchange less meaningful, because instead of the conversation being a full give and take of ideas, a precious part of it must be spent debunking false impressions. This depletes time, vigour and stamina, postponing or foreclosing the discussion of actual ideas. As such, prejudice constantly interrupts substance with stereotype, the antithesis of promoting intellectual pluralism.

Rauch then presumes that we all tussle on the same—level—playing field. In a society where the most hideous and hurtful remarks can be tossed around, he suggests, everybody who takes offence may chirp up, set the record straight and bathe in the glow of truth over tirade. Talk about utopianism. He neglects the reality that patterns of prejudice lead many people to consider themselves inferior and therefore not worthy of being heard. They often do not, because they cannot, respond to more caricature, slander or hate. In effect, their freedom of expression is curbed by others' abuse of this right. Leaving the power imbalance intact does not guarantee a flow of ideas; it might just ensure their blockage.

Even where inferiority complexes are not involved, the combination of power and prejudice can stop its targets from speaking their minds. Recently, a man followed my girfriend and me down a bustling Toronto street in the afternoon sunshine. He was yelling ideas (or were they impressions?) about what he figured she and I did in our private moments. My gut warned me that physical violence would be his next move if either of us reacted to him. In an effort to prevent an assault, we shut ourselves up—a seriously grudging sacrifice for me. Our freedom of speech gave way to someone else's, and the responsibility to contain violence lay with *us*, not him. This was not intellectual pluralism. It was verbal terrorism— "ideas" through intimidation.

By condoning prejudice as a badge of diversity, Rauch ultimately undermines diversity. If you really do not care to hear others, then in his society you are entitled to cruise on the automatic pilot of stereotype. The convenience of stereotyping becomes a right. As a result, it becomes a cop-out, too.

In urging that informed judgement prevail over prejudice, I want to further a Utopia of Complexity, where we do not know what we will get until we give each other the time of day. "[W]e all need comfort zones," Dana Putnam acknowledges from her experience in women's studies classes, "but if we get too comfortable, that means somebody has figured it all out and we're just absorbing it instead of creating it." *Creating it*. A world that defeats prejudice with informed judgement allows us to be innovative because our thoughts are not boiled down to our biological profiles.

In this utopia, white feminists need not attribute racial rancour to challenges from feminists of colour, and feminists of colour have no reason to regard all white feminists with latent mistrust. Credibility, like beauty, is more than skin deep.

In this utopia, gays and lesbians may vote conservative without straight cons steering clear in homophobic horror, or queer progressives disavowing their presumed "brothers and sisters" as punishment for high treason.

In this utopia, Canadian federalists and Quebec separatists take their cues from a common dislike of caricature. Ron Graham explains in his 1996 essay to fellow journalists, "Using Power Well":

> We all know the joke: You can always pick out the federalist at a Quebec dinner party; just look for the guest who doesn't say anything ... That silent guest, however, does have something that unites him or her with both the separatists at the table and every single one of us: We all hate being dismissed and excluded because of a simplistic, generalized, often negative stereotype of who we are and what we think ... Not to know about our differences, not to study their complexities, not to try to transcend the barriers and communicate would be to miss the biggest story of all—the story of life.

In that vein, to choose prejudice over informed judgement might be to miss the real action. Perhaps better conceived as "premature articulation," prejudice robs not only the conversational partner, but oneself, of any memorable moment. The human impulse to judge is not squelched in the Utopia of Complexity; it is made socially productive, as Jonathan Rauch would want it, by constant exchanges between civic equals.

That means the Utopia of Complexity will be an unholy mess for purists—religious, ideological or otherwise. They will not take kindly to more education of the sort conducted last year by Ontario's Addiction Research Foundation (ARF). A video subtitled "The Street Youth's Guide to Fun and Safe Drug Use" advises viewers to: Never use the same needle twice; build trust with a single needle supplier; switch from heroin to methadone; be polite to police if you want them to leave you alone; and go to a shelter when you overdose. Morally bankrupt? Perhaps. But ethically stocked to the hilt.

Replacing morals, which are absolute, with ethics, which respond to changing situations, could be the pragmatic price of genuine civic interaction. "If we want to talk to people and engage in dialogue," says ADF president Perry Kendall, "we have to talk the way they want to be talked to." That is why his foundation tried "participatory research and development"; youth with street experience shot the video. One verdict: "[T]he work they created," pronounced *Globe and Mail* reporter John Allemang, "is funny and insightful about drug use and more critical of spaced-out druggies and dumb drunks than perhaps even the non-judgmental addiction researchers intended." Surprises all around.

At the same time, order matters. None of us wakes up every day and shouts "Surprise me!" because a completely unpatterned society would be terrifying. However, my utopia knows the difference between chaos and complexity: *chaos is complexity without the exercise of mutual obligation.* What orders the Utopia of Complexity, then, are the values of empathy, agency and accountability. With the breakdown of territorial borders—our traditional conduits of identity—the nation needs new organizing principles. Can we rely on technology? No; as I have tried to show, technology harbours no ethical awareness. Values, on the other hand, shape what we can do with technology, how we can view each other in our specific struggles for justice and, in wider society, what we can change and where we can accept change. In short, values let us imagine the possibilities of being human.

I recognize the possibility that people need to be wary of an "other"; the variable is how that wariness gets channelled. In this age of protean, often invisible, threats to identity, neo-cons shrewdly give voters a package not just of personal values but also of accessible enemies—immigrants, single parents, welfare recipients. In Ontario, after tepid mutterings of "love and solidarity" from a premier named Rae, after his government's ads condemning violence against women, after pay equity, employment equity and an attempt (however half-hearted) at same-sex spousal benefits, people were again allowed to loathe under the Mike Harris conservatives. From the constipation of civility to the diarrhea of demonization: what a relief it was. What a landslide it was.

But even if human beings need to fear, and even though we need to plumb meaning from our minor differences, I doubt that we need to cling to an us-against-them morality. The hints abound in the stories of my co-travellers, in the Canadian public's hunger for a new social covenant and in the emerging generation's flexibility, as documented by Michael Adams. Consider, too, the daily decisions of powerful and less-than-powerful people around the world.

There is the grace with which South African president Nelson Mandela has treated his prison guard of more than two decades, James Gregory. In his 1996 memoir, *Goodbye Bafana*, Gregory published the note that Mandela penned on the day of his release. "You will always be in my thoughts," the internationally beloved prisoner wrote to his warden. "Meantime I send and your family fond regards and best wishes." Mandela later invited Gregory to his presidential inauguration as well as the opening of parliament. The intent of reconciling "us" with "them" could not have been more plain. Indeed, in encouraging a national speak-out on human rights atrocities committed during the apartheid years, Mandela has established a travelling commission whose title accords equal weight to "Truth" and "Reconciliation."

The flimsy shacks of Soweto township still stand alongside racial suspicions in South Africa. But with each of his overtures, Mandela has conveyed that the matter of peace is bigger than *my* pain and *your* guilt. Unwilling to buckle to blame, his example has kept a huge, historically divided country in relatively orderly transition.

Then again, that is Saint Nelson. A lesser-known conciliator is Rosa Goldenberg. In July 1996, the *Toronto Star* reported that this Holocaust survivor would be honouring a Belgian woman whose family sheltered her during World War Two. Although Goldenberg's parents, brother and sister were gassed by the Nazis, the Jewish grandmother cannot bring herself to bitterness. "I long to have known my mother," the *Star* quotes her as saying. "I'd love to have remembered her loving me. But I refuse to hate." Like Mandela, Goldenberg consciously decided to make peace with her past, telling us that polarization—with its knack for vigilante therapy— is not inevitable.

Polarization might not even be instinctive: nature is home to a relentless give and take between creatures. Whatever thrill humans get from ascribing a hunt-or-be-hunted, eat-or-be-eaten duality to their behaviour, animals coexist in an intricate web of emotions and ethics. Having studied the evolution of empathy, Emory University scientist Frans B. M. de Waal points to "many instances of animals caring for one another" out of self-interest—"evidence so rich that it seems to prove that survival depends not only on strength and combat but also at times on co-operation and kindness." Complexity is the energy of this universe. To learn from it, we cannot seek to dominate it; we must flow within it.

Flow with a measure of control. To that end, empathy, agency and accountability can provide the interior unity—the "order of the soul" to repeat Leonard Cohen's gorgeous phrase—that helps to balance out the fragmentation of our external world. It goes far to reknit the individual to the community. With these values, we can personalize order, influencing our relationships but also being influenced by them. The result is control without domination.

A vision of mass political transformation and a prescription for inner order: have I tumbled into the authoritarianism that Jonathan Rauch detects in dreamers like me? If so, therein lies the crowning paradox of my journey. I reach for a society where people are indoctrinated to be non-doctrinaire, where negotiation is the only non-negotiable and where we all embody the same basic values precisely so that we may express our unique individual selves. Authoritarianism does not get much more accommodating. Yet that is the distinction of norms in the Utopia of Complexity—they bend in the service of belonging.

Paradox has been a faithful companion on my journey. Once a pugilist of identity politics, I now understand that our universe is too inchoate for mere labels. Belonging needs labels as tarmacs, and then it needs to move past labels in a negotiated navigation to identity. Hence my new respect for liberalism, by which I mean an openness to learn and to marshall those lessons to practical ends. Defined this way, liberalism is as much a philosophy of Thich Nhat Hanh as of Jean Jacques Rousseau; a historic, borderless pursuit of discovery which, when adapted to post-modern times, brings us to the mind-blowing realization that we know too much to stop educating ourselves now. Given its embrace of curiosity, liberalism eschews dogma. It needs democracy.

But at a time of institutional breakdown and territorial blurring, democracy is being bled of meaning. To regain relevance, democracy literally has to be radicalized: its roots deepened; its ingredients transplanted in the very soil of society, the individual; and the invitation to negotiate extended so that every individual may be a participant, even if her labels announce an apparent deviant. This radical democracy, emerging from a culture of interaction, leading to an ethos of belonging, would cultivate a virtual nation that I have called the Utopia of Complexity. Were we all civic equals in the Utopia of Complexity, we would be allowed to transcend our biology, obliged to negotiate identity, free—I dare say— to claim a controlling interest in our destiny.

Dare is the operative word. While believing that it provides more hope than the alternatives, I do not claim this dream to be the Answer. To gamble on it is to risk what we already have. Not to try it is to risk complacency amid an accelerating wave of polarization. I have not plugged all the holes in the dike of my utopia; there are more than a few leaks in logic. But as Michael Ignatieff notes, "Modern secular humanism is empty if it supposes that the human good is without internal contradiction. These contradictions cannot be resolved in principle, only in practice."

In this case, practice makes imperfect. Let us get on with it.

ENDNOTES

Each reference is identified by the last few words of the sentence, or cluster of sentences, in which it appears.After citing the reference once,I have used my discretion about whether future references from the same source warrant another citation.The reader will find that I err on the side of avoiding repetition—except in the rare case where I have used more than one work by the same author.

INTRODUCTION

"... enter into the hearts of even those who [are] different." Gordon Wood quoted by Edward Tivnan, *The Moral Imagination: Confronting the Ethical Issues of Our Day*. (New York: Touchstone, 1995)

CHAPTER ONE

"... beneath difference there is identity." Michael Ignatieff, *The Needs of Strangers:An Essay on Privacy, Solidarity, and the Politics of Being Human*. (London: Chatto & Windus, 1984)

"... and from which we cannot escape." Jean-Marie Guéhenno (translated by Victoria Elliott), *The End of the Nation-State*. (Minneapolis: University of Minnesota Press, 1995)

"... not for the business class." Judy Rebick, speech to public forum on "Rebuilding the Left." (Toronto, November 1995)

"... retreat to Palm Springs in their search for belonging." Douglas Coupland, *Generation X:Tales for an Accelerated Culture*. (New York: St. Martin's Press, 1991)

"... "eulogy" for his concept of Generation X." Douglas Coupland, "Generation X'd." *Details* (June 1995)

" ... why did you tell me it was filled?" Lee Maracle quoting her daughter, "Ramparts Hanging in the Air," in The Telling Book Collective, eds., *Telling It:Women and Language across Cultures*. (Vancouver: Press Gang Publishers, 1990)

"... and then slices through all of us on the rebound." Donna Laframboise, *The Princess at the Window:A New Gender Morality*. (Toronto: Penguin, 1996)

"... no mainstream movement to join." Rene Denfeld, *The New Victorians:A Young Woman's Challenge to the Old Feminist Order*. (New York:Warner Books, 1995)

"... a feminist who doesn't like what feminism has become." Christina Hoff Sommers,

Who Stole Feminism? How Women Have Betrayed Women. (New York: Simon & Schuster, 1994)

"... body of the women's movement." Susan Faludi, "I'm Not a Feminist But I Play One on TV." *Ms.* (March/April 1995)

CHAPTER TWO

Major sources are author interviews with Joanne St. Lewis (Toronto, 1994, and by phone, 1996) and Sunera Thobani (Toronto, 1994 and 1996).

"... none of us is one-dimensional." Kim Campbell, interview on *Petrie in Prime*, CBC Newsworld. (July 31, 1995)

"... equal players in national political life." Margaret Wente, "She's a pioneer, but is she good at governing?" *Globe and Mail* (June 15, 1993)

"... tiny club of CEOs is a major breakthrough." Margaret Wente, "Women in power, and the paths they took." *Globe and Mail* (July 9, 1994)

"... choose to seduce him." Kate Fillion, *Lip Service:The Truth about Women's Darker Side in Love, Sex, and Friendship.* (Toronto: HarperCollins, 1996)

"... matters little what your title is." Kim Campbell, *Time and Chance:The Political Memoirs of Canada's First Woman Prime Minister.* (Toronto: Doubleday Canada Ltd., 1996)

"... gender-specific aspects of our personality are not." Kim Campbell, speech at Women in the Media conference. (Ottawa, November 1992)

"... tried to smuggle feminism into everything on the ed board." Susan Riley, presentation at Women in the Media Conference. (Vancouver, November 1991)

"Territory and toys." Catherine Ford, author interview. (Calgary, 1994)

"... I had to ask myself, 'Am I happy?' " Catherine Ford quoted by Kimberley Prince, "Wild Rose: Beneath the Thorny Exterior of an Old-style Columnist Lies a Softer Side That Few People Are Allowed to See," *Ryerson Review of Journalism.* (Spring 1995)

"... Canadian citizenship has ceased to have any value." Anonymous correspondent quoted in "Backlash." *Leaf Lines* (Volume 5, Number 3, Summer 1993)

"... different race and tongue than our own." Nellie McClung quoted by Mary Hallett and Marilyn Davis, *Firing the Heather:The Life and Times of Nellie McClung.* (Saskatoon: Fifth House, 1993)

"... abortion rights movement in B.C. today." Joy Thompson quoted by Anjula Gogia, "From Rebick to Thobani: NAC gets a new head." *Kinesis* (May 1993)

"... all came from female journalists." Susan Riley, "Feminist meeting brings out differences." *Ottawa Citizen* (June 15, 1994)

"... culture which tends to absorb women." Rosemary Speirs quoted by Elizabeth Jerch, "Making Up New Rules." *Reports from Women in the Media 1992:Special Bulletin of the Canadian Association of Journalists* (January 1993)

"... shrill little interest groups." Janice Kennedy, "When NAC stormed Parliament, did it really know where it was going?" *Ottawa Citizen* (June 17, 1994)

"... increasingly narrow in its representation." Michael Valpy, "Two major fears about the social-policy debate." *Globe and Mail* (October 5, 1994)

"... fight has to be for jobs." Sunera Thobani quoted by Janet McFarland, "Sunera Thobani a quiet force of conviction." *Financial Post* (July 10, 1993)

"... important that a woman of colour head NAC." Sunera Thobani, "NAC must fight racism, wherever found." *Toronto Star* (July 4, 1996)

CHAPTER THREE

"... at least on its own rhetorical terms." Reg Whitaker, "Sovereign Division: Quebec Nationalism Between Liberalism and Ethnicity," in James Littleton, ed., *Clash of Identities: Essays on Media, Manipulation and Politics of the Self*. (Toronto: Canadian Broadcasting Company/Prentice-Hall, 1996)

"... identity politics as a 'new primitivism.' " John Fekete, *Moral Panic: Biopolitics Rising*. (Montreal: Robert Davies Publishing, 1994)

"... more to demographics than to any personal failings." David K. Foot and Daniel Stoffman, *Boom, Bust & Echo: How to Profit from the Coming Demographic Shift*. (Toronto: Macfarlane Walter & Ross, 1996)

"... all kinds of other women's experiences compare" and "something like *Girls Like Me?*" Kate Fillion and H. S. Bhabra, interview on *Imprint*, TVOntario. (February 4, 1996)

"... burn each other's property." George Bush quoted by Edward Tivnan, *The Moral Imagination: Confronting the Ethical Issues of Our Day*. (New York: Touchstone, 1995)

"Now that I seek myself, I find God." Beyazid Bestami quoted by Ali Shari'ati (translated by R. Campbell), *Marxism and Other Western Fallacies: An Islamic Critique*. (Berkeley: Mizan Press, 1980)

"... the phrase English Canada has become politically incorrect." Richard Gwyn, *Nationalism without Walls: The Unbearable Lightness of Being Canadian*. (Toronto: McClelland & Stewart, 1995)

"... dividing things as a means of control." Marshall McLuhan, *Understanding Media: The Extensions of Man*, revised edition. (New York: McGraw-Hill, 1965)

"... the belief that the self is formed in opposition to another." bell hooks, *Feminist Theory: From Margin to Center*. (Boston: South End Press, 1984)

"... wholly negative experience for women." Caroline Ramazanoglu, *Feminism and the Contradictions of Oppression*. (London: Routledge, 1989)

"... no-win situation for women." Audrey McLaughlin in remarks on *Face Off*, CBC Newsworld. (December 2, 1994)

"... isn't going to advance [the feminist] cause." Heather Robertson, "Sharpe tales of women in the bitchy game of politics" (review of Sydney Sharpe's *The Gilded Ghetto*). *Globe and Mail* (November 19, 1994)

"... topple the class system." Quoted from official document of former Yugoslavia by Maxine Molyneux, "Women in Socialist Societies: Problems of Theory and Practice," in Kate Young et al., eds., *Of Marriage and the Market: Women's Subordination Internationally and Its Lessons*. (London: Routledge & Kegan Paul, 1984)

"... it was due to family responsibilities." Quoted from Cuban document by Muriel Nazzari, "The 'Woman Question' in Cuba: An Analysis of Material Constraints on Its Solution." *Signs: Journal of Women in Culture and Society* (Volume 9, Number 21, 1983)

"... 'growing' at rates faster than their wealthy counterparts." Lester Brown et al., *Vital Signs 1994: The Trends That Are Shaping Our Future*. (Washington, D.C.: WorldWatch Institute/W. W. Norton & Co., 1994)

"The global economy is changing that." David Suzuki, "Economics no measure of progress."
  Toronto Star (August 5, 1995)

"... designed to stand the test of time." Pat Carney quoted by Christopher Waddell,
  "Carney unconcerned that free trade deal will bind future policy." *Globe and Mail*
  (October 30, 1987)

"... very things that made them successful." Fred Bienefeld, author interviews. (Toronto,
  1995 and Ottawa, 1996)

"... fall in line behind a more open agenda" and "dictate terms to the rest of the world."
  Clayton Yeutter and Mahathir bin Mohamad quoted by Madelaine Drohan, "A partnership of wealth?" *Globe and Mail* (July 15, 1995)

"... risks of a spiral of rising intolerance are enormous." Michael Ignatieff, "The Narcissism of
  Minor Difference," in James Littleton, ed., *Clash of Identities:Essays on Media,Manipulation
  and Politics of the Self* (Toronto: Canadian Broadcasting Company / Prentice-Hall, 1996)

INTRODUCTION TO SECTION TWO

"... last vestige of external influence." Robert Bellah et al., *Habits of the Heart:Individualism
  and Commitment in American Life.* (Berkeley: University of California Press, 1985)

"... more a matter of rational calculation." Richard Rorty, "What's Wrong With 'Rights.' "
  Harper's (June 1996)

"... stability and security characterize both camps." George Lakoff, *Moral Politics:What
  Conservatives Know That Liberals Don't.* (Chicago: University of Chicago Press, 1996)

"... de-spiritualization of daily life." Michael Lerner, *The Politics of Meaning:Restoring Hope
  and Possibility in an Age of Cynicism.* (New York: Addison-Wesley, 1996)

CHAPTER FOUR

Major sources are author interviews with Tzeporah Berman (Vancouver, 1995) and Afra
  and Mariam Jalabi (Montreal, 1994; by phone, 1996).

"... public forest will be back in the hands of the public." Tzeporah Berman quoted by
  Deborah Wilson, "Taking a stand for the Sound." *Globe and Mail* (August 14, 1993)

"... atmosphere of calm and dignity." Tzeporah Berman, "Takin' It Back," in *Clayoquot &
  Dissent:Essays.* (Vancouver: Ronsdale Press, 1994)

"... with interculturalism you have a common state." Madelaine Lussier quoted by
  Amber Nasrulla, "Educators outside Quebec mystified by hijab ban." *Globe and Mail*
  (December 14, 1994)

CHAPTER FIVE

Major sources are author interviews with Thomas Ponniah (Toronto, 1995 and 1996) and
  Trudy Parsons (St. John's, 1994, and by phone, 1996).

"Personal renewal is the route to success." William Thorsell, "Despite the Republicans'
  'American dream,' the U.S. is clearly fragmented." *Globe and Mail* (August 17, 1996)

"... departs wildly from indulging in 'rights talk.' " Richard Rorty, "What's Wrong With
  'Rights.' " *Harper's* (June 1996)

"... framing her thin, serious face." John de Mont, "Love and Fear in the Age of AIDS."
  Maclean's (February 22, 1993)

CHAPTER SIX

Major sources are author interviews with Nicole Soucey (Ottawa, 1995, and by phone, 1996); Karen Pederson (Cutknife, 1994, and by phone, 1996); Dana Putnam (Vancouver, 1994, and by phone, 1996) and Claire Huang Kinsley (Toronto, 1995 and 1996).

"... a waning of respect from family and friends." James Laxer, *In Search of a New Left: Canadian Politics after the Neo-Conservative Assault.* (Toronto: Viking, 1996)

"... legal partnership agreements between husband and wife." Francis Shaver, "Farm Women and Agriculture: An Overview of Issues." January 1991 paper distributed by Farm Women's Bureau

CHAPTER SEVEN

Major sources are author interviews with Sadia Zaman (Toronto, 1994, 1995 and 1996) and the Women's Constituency Group (Charlottetown, 1994, and Lori Duckworth by phone, 1996).

"... quadrupled in the last quarter century to two million." Anderson Cooper, *ABC World News Tonight.* (September 21, 1996)

"Sir Rodmond, it is your move." Nellie McClung quoted by Mary Hallett and Marilyn Davis, *Firing the Heather: The Life and Times of Nellie McClung.* (Saskatoon: Fifth House, 1993)

"... no medical or physical evidence to indicate that the victim was beaten." Gerry Birt, "Chronicle of a Crisis." *UPEI Magazine* (Volume 6, Number 4, Autumn 1992)

"... perhaps some violence might have been avoided." Roddy Weatherbee, letter to the editor. *UPEI X-Press* (November 26, 1992)

CHAPTER EIGHT

Major source is author interview with Deborah Tagornak (Toronto, 1995, and by phone, 1996).

"... values like cooperation, generosity, and fellowship." Deborah Tagornak, untitled statement on behalf of Pauktuutit Inuit Women's Association. (Pond Inlet, Northwest Territories: December 8, 1994)

"... encouraged men and women to question." Kathleen Mary Minor, "Elizabeth: An Elder Inuk Remembers Her Life." *Canadian Woman Studies* (Volume 14, Number 4, Fall 1994)

"... and elders will teach young women." Pauktuutit, "Women and Self-Government." Ibid.

"... and only 6 per cent older than fifty-five." Pamela Orr et al., "Aboriginal Women's Health." Ibid.

"... I learned a great deal from her." Martha Flaherty, "Inuit Women: Equality and Leadership." Ibid.

CHAPTER NINE

"... and even of race and gender identity." Michael Adams, *Sex in the Snow: Canadian Social Values at the End of the Millennium.* (Toronto: Viking, 1997)

"... and a way of conducting oneself everyday." Jean Bethke Elshtain, *Democracy on Trial.* (Concord, Ontario: House of Anansi Press, 1993)

"... most educational form of government." Christopher Lasch, "Journalism, Publicity and the Lost Art of Argument." *Media Studies Journal* (Volume 9, Number 1, Winter 1995)

"... in post-Reagan America? Twenty-five times more." Richard Gwyn, *Nationalism without Walls:The Unbearable Lightness of Being Canadian*. (Toronto: McClelland & Stewart, 1996)

"... further destroy one's work ethic and pride." Suzanne Peters, "Exploring Canadian Values: A Synthesis Report." (Ottawa: Canadian Policy Research Network/Renouf Publishing, 1995)

"... we act in ignorance and frustration." Anthony Lewis, "The U.S. welfare bill points to a chilly future." *Globe and Mail* (August 6, 1996; reprinted from *The New York Times*)

"... arrogance fuelled the stock market crash of 1929." Jeremy Rifkin, interview about the future of work on *The National Magazine*, CBC TV (September 4, 1995)

"... viewing audience would pause at the difference." Dwight Drummond, in remarks to forum on International Day to Eliminate Racial Discrimination. (Toronto, March 1996)

"... vendors arguing politics with the stockbrokers." Michael McCarthy, author interview by phone. (1996)

"... the quest to radicalize democracy is alive." Kathy Austin, "Street papers around the world." *Spare Change* (August 1995)

"... we flee towards certainty." John Ralston Saul, *The Unconscious Civilization*. (Concord, Ontario: House of Anansi Press, 1995)

"... easy to open yourself up when you want to." Quoted in Doug Saunders, "E-mail cupids tap out same old love message." *Globe and Mail* (February 14, 1996)

"... responded like Pavlov's dogs." John Doyle, "Blue Screen Effect." *Globe and Mail Broadcast Week* (June 24-30, 1995)

"... has become the primary way of belonging." Jim Wallis, *The Soul of Politics: Beyond "Religious Right"and "Secular Left."* (New York: Harcourt Brace, 1995)

"... vast unseen audience linked by telephone wires." Howard Kurtz, *Hot Air: All Talk All the Time*. (New York: Times Books, 1996)

"... faceless, disembodied 'on-line' self." Derrick de Kerckhove, *The Skin of Culture: Investigating the New Electronic Reality*. (Toronto: Somerville House, 1995)

"... 54 per cent compared to 11." Statistics Canada, Household Facilities and Equipment Survey. *The Daily* (October 23, 1996)

"... 28 per cent of the under-$20,000 crowd can do the same." Jeffrey Frank, "Preparing for the Information Highway: Information Technology in Canadian Households." *Canadian Social Trends* (Statistics Canada, Autumn 1995)

"... yet escaping into distant conversations." Clifford Stoll, *Silicon Snakeoil: Second Thoughts on the Information Highway*. (New York: Doubleday, 1995)

"... with an increased empathy for their students." Neil Postman, *The End of Education: Redefining the Value of School*. (New York: Knopf, 1995)

"... accountable to all those affected by their decisions." Cy Gonick, "Reinventing the Left: Socialism in Canada." *Canadian Dimension* (Volume 28, Number 5, October 1994)

"... expense account and so forth." Lewis Lapham quoted by Andrew Coyne, "A conservative in liberal disguise." *Globe and Mail* (March 15, 1996)

"... a consistent matter of administrative routine." Michael Ignatieff, *The Needs of*

Strangers:An Essay on Privacy, Solidarity, and the Politics of Being Human. (London: Chatto & Windus, 1984)

CHAPTER TEN

"... both Orwellian and hopelessly utopian." Arthur Kroker quoted by Robert Everett-Green, "Humanists get hip to the Net." *Globe and Mail* (June 22, 1996)

"I feel like I'm starting over." Roseanne Barr quoted by Liz Logan, "Roseanne's Biggest Change." *Ladies' Home Journal* (November 1993)

"... the solution looking for problems." Quoted from speech by Augustine Barrios-Gomez, former Mexican ambassador to Canada, verified by embassy spokesperson Jesus Contreras, author interview by phone. (October 1996).

"... I feel like this is what the world should be." Jane Fonda quoted by John Robert Colombo, *Dictionary of Canadian Quotations*. (Toronto: Stoddart, 1991)

"... have access to [MPPs] but the reverse is not true." Morley Kells, "New revolution, old imperialism." *Toronto Star* (July 21, 1995)

"... at the expense of thoughtfulness." George Grant, *Technology and Empire: Perspectives on North America*. (Toronto: House of Anansi, 1969)

"... not necessarily going to be inclusive of everyone." Quoted in Enzo di Matteo, "Accusations, resignations rock alternative radio." *Now* (March 9-15, 1995)

"... can stay the fuck out of my classroom." John Furedy quoted by Michael Keefer, *Lunar Perspectives: Field Notes from the Culture Wars*. (Concord, Ontario: House of Anansi Press, 1996)

"... defends his own group's charitable tax status." Rosemary Speirs, "Right-wing institute is politically correct charity." *Toronto Star* (January 25, 1996)

"... polarization as 'the crack of politics.' " Robert Hughes, *Culture of Complaint: The Fraying of America*. (New York: Warner Books, 1993)

"... same prejudice, namely that of whoever is in authority." Jonathan Rauch, "In Defence of Prejudice: Why Incendiary Speech Must Be Protected." *Harper's* (May 1995)

"... miss the biggest story of all—the story of life." Ron Graham, "Using Power Well," in James Littleton, ed., *Clash of Identities: Essays on Media, Manipulation and Politics of the Self*. (Toronto: Canadian Broadcasting Company/Prentice-Hall, 1996)

"... the non-judgmental addiction researchers intended." John Allemang, "Video teaches safe drug use." *Globe and Mail* (July 17, 1996)

"... fond regards and best wishes." Nelson Mandela quoted by James Gregory, *Goodbye Bafana: Nelson Mandela, My Prisoner, My Friend*. (London: Headline, 1995)

"But I refuse to hate." Rosa Goldenberg quoted by Kathleen Goldhar, "Holocaust survivor reunited with woman who saved her." *Toronto Star* (July 13, 1996)

"... also at times on co-operation and kindness." Frans B. M. de Waal, "Survival of the kindest." *Globe and Mail* (August 23, 1996; reprinted from *The New York Times*)

"... cannot be resolved in principle, only in practice." Michael Ignatieff, *The Needs of Strangers: An Essay on Privacy, Solidarity, and the Politics of Being Human*. (London: Chatto & Windus, 1984)

ACKNOWLEDGEMENTS

About a year after I began researching this book, I told a friend that I could not wait to write the acknowledgements. It would mean I was finished. I now know better than to expect—or desire—an intellectual voyage to end.

I gratefully acknowledge Michael Ignatieff and Jean-Marie Guéhenno, on whose work I have relied heavily and in more ways than one. Whenever I felt listless at the computer, I would only need to read a page or two of their books to get charged up again. There is a word for that kind of impact: inspiration.

Barbara Clarke provided the idea that got this entire ball rolling; Barbara Pulling then scooped up the ball and brought it to Douglas & McIntyre. The Canada Council and the Toronto Arts Council came next with financial assistance. I hope my fellow taxpayers find this book a testament to the promise of public arts funding.

Much of that money went to travel, such as the sixty-hour round-trip bus ride north. Many thanks to the young rabble-rousers at Women's Place Kenora—Ally, Bobby, Natacha, Meghan, Tammy—who made my first set of interviews well worth Greyhound hell. Back home, Patience Elabor-Idemudia let me observe her women's studies class, tolerating my travel-induced absences and whetting my appetite for more knowledge.

Enter my case studies. Everyone who helped me contact the women and men profiled in these pages gets my gratitude. So do those who picked me up, and put me up, during my cross-Canada trek. Of special mention is Catherine Ford, who drove to the rescue when I suddenly needed a place to sleep in Calgary. Liberal with generosity yet in-Kleined to boost Alberta at every turn, Ford also fed me a decadent steak dinner. I thank her for going the extra mile. As for those who agreed to be profiled, they have my profound appreciation and admiration.

Although introduced to this project late, my new agent, Dean Cooke, instantly took to the book, negotiated the thorny nuances of publishing it and salvaged my sanity. I adore his professionalism. Meanwhile, my intellectual mentors, especially Wodek Szemberg, asked me tough questions and told me no lies about the need to think. Their incessant challenges compelled me to reconsider not only my answers but also my questions. With editorial prowess, Maya Mavjee and Clive Thompson pulled a book out of a collection of question marks. Clive's punch complemented Maya's composure, so that I bounced off the walls with a measure of dignity. Ann Bains, Stephen McCammon, Gordon McLennan, Thomas Ponniah, Jeannelle Laillou Savona, Larry Till and Victoria Wilcox, among others, read incarnations of the manuscript—"the God-forsaken manuscript," as I later called it. The interest displayed by each of these people went far to sustain me spiritually.

I owe my deepest debts to those who have shown me the faith of true friendship. Anju Gogia, Sara Borins, Nancy Singh and Margaret Hagemen begin that list: Anju for her loving embraces; Sara for her well-timed pep talks and excellent practical advice; Nancy for being close even if the phone bills dissent; and Margaret for her kindred curiosity, raging intellect and raunchy humanitarianism. Laughing with her is a serious lesson in healthy living. A bear hug as well to Mendelson Joe, whose constant correspondence reminded me that we really can care about one another as citizens.

Finally, the family: my sisters Ish and Fatima, and their respective partners Marlon Lyons and Derrick McClinton, never doubted my abilities. But they knew my frailties enough not to inquire, "Isn't that book done yet?" Their pressure-free support was invaluable. Above all, Mumtaz Mawji has taught me more than Marshall McLuhan about communication. In my moments of silent despair, her notes, cards and calls made the difference. Thanks, Mum.

INDEX

IRSHAD MANJI is a writer and broadcaster living in Toronto. A widely sought-after commentator on social, political and cultural issues, she has been named by *Maclean's* magazine as one of "100 Leaders of Tomorrow." Previously national affairs editorial writer for the *Ottawa Citizen* and former co-star of the TVOntario debate show *Friendly Fire*, she now produces and hosts "In the Public Interest," an investigative feature on Vision TV's flagship human affairs program *Skylight*.